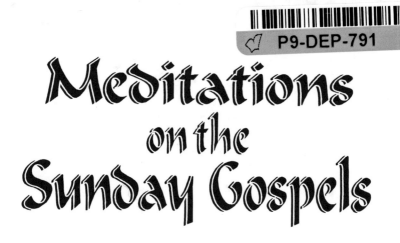

Meditations
on the
Sunday Gospels

Meditations on the Sunday Gospels

Year A

compiled and edited by
John E. Rotelle, O.S.A.

New City Press

Published in the United States by New City Press
202 Cardinal Rd., Hyde Park, NY 12538
©1995 Augustinian Heritage Institute

Library of Congress Cataloging-in-Publication Data:

  Meditations on the Sunday Gospels / introduced and edited by John E.
  Rotelle.

    Includes bibliographical references and index.
    Contents: [1] Year A.
    ISBN 1-56548-032-5 (v. 1 : pbk.)
    1. Church year meditations. 2. Bible. N.T. Gospels
  —Meditations. 3. Catholic Church—Prayer-books and devotions
  —English.   I. Rotelle, John E.
  BX2170.C55M43   1995
  242'.3—dc20   95-9013

Printed in the United States of America

To

Sister Margarita, O.D.C.

An Everlasting Tribute

Sister Margaret Brady was born into an English Catholic family in 1908. An intelligent and gifted child she won, at the age of 17, a State scholarship to Saint Thomas' Hall at Mount Pleasant University. To the consternation of her tutors, however, she renounced her academic career after only two years so as to enter the Carmelite Order as a nun. As it happened another young woman and friend of Margarita's followed the same course of action at about the same time and such was the impact made by the decision of these two that, it is said, the University Senate convened to propose that Catholic girls should not be awarded scholarships since they could not be relied upon to honor their commitment!

Sister Margarita's chosen vocation might not have seemed at first to have allowed much scope for her undoubted intellectual gifts. Her life of hidden dedication, however, did not allow them to be wasted. An excellent Latinist, she was selected to assist in translating for the ICEL version of the revised Roman Breviary. She also wrote hymns and poems many of which were also published for liturgical use. The present collection of readings owes much to her enthusiasm and energy as also to her determination that women writers should be adequately represented. She died of cancer in 1984.

Contents

Foreword

From the earliest days of Christianity there has always been an emphasis on reading. The New Testament was written so that people would be able to reflect on it; from century to century it was copied and brought to other parts of the world. The writings of the Greek, Latin, Syriac, and other Church writers were also copied and transported from monastery to monastery, from city to city, from country to country. All this was done so that people would have access to the wisdom and insights of these Church writers.

With an anthology of readings you do much the same thing. You take the best of Church writers over the centuries and present these excellent and timely writings to posterity.

In this present collection of readings I selected those readings which best accompany the gospel passage for each Sunday of the three-year cycle of gospel readings and which convey some kind of message for our day and age. The reading is aligned with each gospel passage which is given in summary form at the very beginning. At times the gospel passage has one theme; where there are several themes in the gospel passage, a choice of one theme or other has to be made. The reading is not a commentary, in the strict sense, on the gospel; the reading was selected as a reflection, meditation, or elongation of the gospel.

I purposely stayed within the framework of what historians call the modern era—seventeenth to the twentieth centuries. At times I did select, by way of exception, some readings from earlier centuries. My reason for staying within this framework is twofold: First, I wanted to emphasize the importance of the modern era and that tradition is ongoing and does not just stop with the Fathers of the Church; secondly, I respected what has already been published, for example, *Journey with the Fathers*,[1] which is along the lines of this

---

1. E. Barnecut, ed., *Journey with the Fathers*, Year A, B, C (Hyde Park: New City Press, 1992-94).

book with a heavy emphasis on Church writers, and *Tradition Day by Day*,[2] readings for each day of the year from Church writers.

Lectio Divina

When we hear the word "reading," we immediately think of taking up a newspaper, magazine, or book and reading through it for information or for enjoyment. This is one type of reading. However, there is another type of reading in the Church's tradition, in which one reads not for information, although this may come with the reading, nor for enjoyment, although this can be present, but for the enrichment of the inner spirit. It is a type of reading that is a prayer in itself; you are (or seem to be) reading, but actually you are praying. The patristic texts in particular lend themselves to this type of reading because they are filled with quotes from scripture or with scriptural allusions. But some modern readings can elicit the same.

Thus, in reading such texts, you are feeding the inner spirit and you are praying. In addition, the texts prompt many beautiful thoughts, ideas, and prayers. One cannot just read the text and put it aside; the text stays with you and leads you to greater depths of thought and prayer. This is *lectio divina*—literally, divine or sacred reading.

A medieval writer in the book *Meditations of Saint Augustine* depicts well this notion of *lectio divina*:

> I love to raise the eyes of my heart to you, elevate my mind to you, and shape the affections of my soul to harmonize with you. I love to speak and hear and write and converse about you, daily to read of your glorious blessedness, and frequently to mull over in my heart what I have read of you. In this way I am able to turn from the passions and dangers and labors of this mortal and transitory life to the sweet coolness of your life-giving breezes and, when I so turn, to rest my weary head, even if only for a moment, on your bosom. It is for this purpose that I enter the pleasing fields of the sacred scriptures, there to find and pluck

---

2. J. E. Rotelle, ed., *Tradition Day by Day* (Villanova: Augustinian Press, 1994).

the fresh growth of its sentences, to eat by reading and digest by frequent meditation, and finally to gather them all into the deep storehouse of my memory.

How To Use This Book

One could pick up this book and read it from cover to cover, but I doubt if that person would derive much from that reading. The best way to use this book is twofold: First, you could read it in conjunction with the Sunday gospel in the proper cycle, that is, Year A, B, or C. Or, secondly, one who preaches could use it as background for a homily or sermon; others could use it in preparation for the Sunday celebration. The book could be used as a source of meditation either for each Sunday, or in preparation for the Sunday, or for some days during the year.

Inclusive Language

The readings range from the seventeenth to the twentieth centuries. Some are translations; others were written in English—English of different eras, a Cardinal Newman English to a Gerald Vann style.

Wherever possible, inclusive language has been the goal without detriment, however, to the meaning. At times it was easy, changing man to human being, men to men and women; at other times it was not so easy, and at times changes could not be made because the male or female (as in the case of Julian of Norwich) imagery was embedded in the text.

The Dedication

I would be remiss if I did not say something about the person to whom I dedicated this book, Sister Margarita of the Order of Discalced Carmelite Nuns. I never met her in person; I only knew her through letters. In a letter written to me when we first began work on the alternative lectionary for the Liturgy of the Hours she, at that time a woman in her seventies, could not emphasize enough the importance of modern readings in the collection. Time and time again she sent me texts, excellent texts, as proposals for the alternative lectionary. Unfortunately, the committee did not agree with her. However, I always had the desire to publish such a book.

Not only was she an advocate of modern readings as a continuity of tradition, but she was years ahead of her time with regard to what we now call inclusive language.

I always admired the strength and "modernity" in her letters and am grateful for her steadfastness in emphasizing the continuance of tradition in all centuries.

I would like to thank those who read the manuscript for me and offered helpful suggestions to improve it: Michael F. Di Gregorio, Francis J. Horn, O.S.A., Gillian Leslie, O.D.C., and Patricia Lo.

It is my hope that this florilegium of texts will help you to deepen your living of the gospel life and to provide you with moments of prayerful reading and revelation.

John E. Rotelle, O.S.A.

Readings

First Sunday of Advent

Gospel: Matthew 24:37-44 Jesus said to his disciples: "As it was in Noah's day, so will it be when the Son of Man comes. For in those days before the flood people were eating, drinking, taking wives, taking husbands, right up to the day Noah went into the ark."

Commentary: J. Pinsk

Advent means coming, the coming of the Lord. If we want to celebrate Advent with the Church, we must first seek to understand what this means: "God is coming." The word "coming" may be regarded as one of the primordial words in the language of religion, for if religion is the loving and unifying encounter with God, it can only be realized when God comes. Unfortunately the same thing happens with God's coming to us as with his loving us—in both cases we want to take the second step before the first one. We think that we must love God first so that he will love us first; and yet, in his first letter Saint John states expressly, *Here is love, not that we loved God, but that he loved us.* Yes, we must love God because he first loved us. We cannot come to God unless he first comes to us. This coming of God is not merely an interior, spiritual affair; it happens rather in palpable, concrete forms. So the coming of God has the same meaning as the revelation of God. Those, therefore, who carefully read and contemplate the words of holy scripture, which are a sign of his continued and continuous coming, will not find it difficult to understand that the actual content of scripture is the proclamation of the coming of God. His coming is the key to the history of the Old Testament and the basic theme of its people, but this is only a prelude to that coming of God in which the Word was made flesh.

All these are ideas with which we are very familiar, so familiar in fact that we tend to think that everything has already been fulfilled. God has come in Jesus Christ; through him he is with us in his grace by faith and the sacraments. Each individual Christian personally, and the Church of Christ as a community, is a sign of the fact that God

16

has come and is with us forever. *Lo, I am with you always, even to the end of the world.* These are the words of our Lord at the end of Saint Matthew's gospel.

We Christians today are so conscious of the joy of our belief in the presence of the Lord, above all in the eucharist, that we almost forget that Christ himself continued to speak of his coming right up to the end of his earthly life, even though he was already present. He spoke of a further coming, beyond the Church and the sacraments.

Although the One who is to come has already appeared, the New Testament, like the Old, is full of the promise and expectation of a new coming of Christ. The gospels speak of it, so do the apostolic letters, and most of all the Revelation of Saint John. This final book of the Bible teaches us: *The Spirit and the Bride say, "Come." Let him who hears say: "Come."* He who testifies to these things says: *Yes, indeed, I am coming soon* and the congregation of the faithful cries out once more: *Come, Lord Jesus!*

(*Gedanken zum Herrenjahr*, 162-164)

Johannes Pinsk (1891-1957) was ordained in 1915 and was, successively, secretary to his bishop, religious instructor in Breslau, student chaplain in Berlin, and pastor in the Berlin suburb of Lankwitz. Pinsk came under the influence of the monks of Maria Laach, especially the abbot Ildefons Herwegen and the theologian Odo Casel. A spiritual leader in Berlin and a very popular speaker, Pinsk devoted his life to explaining the liturgy and bringing others to love it. His great concern was the image of the risen Christ and the Easter mystery, the experience of the Church as a worshiping community, and the consecration of the world through the sacramental life.

Second Sunday of Advent

Gospel: Matthew 3:1-12

In those days, John the Baptist appeared; he preached in the wilderness of Judea and this was his message: "Repent, for the kingdom of God is close at hand."

Commentary: C. Lubich

*T*he conversion called for in the gospel by John the Baptist and, immediately after him, by Jesus, consists in a complete reversal of our lifestyle, a real 180 degree turn. It means putting God, rather than self or any other earthly thing, at the center of our life; of making his Word the measure of all our thoughts and actions.

The great sin into which the Pharisees and Sadducees had fallen was exactly that of not having given God his rightful place, easily confusing with their own interpretations what it was that he was actually asking. For example, they placed more importance on all the outward display of religion and its cult (ritual ablutions, Temple sacrifices, rigorous observance of the Sabbath rest etc.) than on what God wanted, especially love of neighbor and service of others. Jesus was to emphasize even more clearly that the will of God consists, in a special way, precisely in this: *Bring forth fruit, then, worthy of repentance.*

To give God first place, to put him at the center of one's life...

But in our day, unfortunately, we note a tendency to avoid God emerging in the modern generation, who is thought of as being too demanding and troublesome. For various reasons people want, quite simply, to eliminate him from their lives as superfluous, as useless. There is a way of looking at things behind this approach which, taking the triumphs of science as its starting point, believes that scientific and technological progress will increase our ability to reach the point of resolving all our problems and mastering the universe by ourselves. Thus the modern generation—and this is its great sin—believes itself to be self-sufficient.

For many people in our era, then, repentance will consist in accepting—or re-accepting—God in their lives; God, without whom we have no real meaning. *Bring forth fruit worthy of repentance, then.*

Another way of evading God for those of today who, nevertheless, believe in him, lies in not knowing how to, or not wanting to, draw the consequences of their faith in the concrete.

The truth is that even we Christians are often able to see ourselves in those Pharisees and Sadducees against whom the Baptist let fly. How often are we Christian more by certain inherited habits and a smattering of religious instruction than by deep conviction and deliberate choice of God! Maybe we reduce our Christianity to its traditions and outward practices without feeling ourselves obliged to put into practice God's commandments, especially that of love of neighbor? But in that case how can we claim that God has first place in our lives? *So bring forth fruit worthy of repentance.*

What shall we do to put the Word of life into practice, then? We must look truthfully at where we stand before Jesus. Some of us, perhaps, ought to welcome with love the Jesus they have excluded from their lives. Others will feel the necessity of considering his demands more seriously. For yet others, who have already set out on this road, it will be a question of renewing their choice of him, if only by means of particular resolutions. What matters is that we should all be converted and converted again.

One thing is certain. Our world that is so wounded can only be healed by Jesus. And he calls on us, his disciples, to allow him to live in us. Baptism has given us his life but our own, freely chosen, living out of it is required: the gospel, with all that it demands, cannot be lived on discount, it cannot be watered down. If we do this we will experience his transforming power. For all of us, then, there is only one thing to do: let us be converted in reality, in deed.

(*From Scripture to Life,* 18-20)

Chiara Lubich (1920-   ), born in Trent, Italy, is the foundress and president of the Focolare whose spirituality of unity has benefited millions of people of all races and cultures. She is a member of the Pontifical Council of the Laity, and a leading figure in world ecumenism. In 1977 she was awarded the Templeton Prize for the progress of religions and currently she is an honorary president of the World Council of Religions for Peace.

Third Sunday of Advent

Gospel: Matthew 11:2-11

Now John in his prison had heard what Christ was doing and sent his disciples to ask him, "Are you the one who is to come, or do we have to wait for someone else?"

Commentary: T. Merton

Christ's answer to the disciples of John was the answer of newness and of life: *Go and tell John what you have seen: the blind see, the lame walk, and the poor have the gospel preached to them.* Here are two kinds of eschatological signs, and they compenetrate one another, for they are all signs of life, proceeding from love. Evil ends, and gives place to good in a physical and visible way: blindness ends, sight begins. Sickness ends, health begins. Death ends, life begins. But all these signs are evidence of an inexhaustible living power, the action of life itself, bursting into time, defeating and reversing the work of time. Hence this power manifests *the fullness of time,* in which time is no longer mere irreversible succession, mere passage from insufficiency to insufficiency. Above all, the raising of the dead is a reversal and a conquest of time: for normally when the "hour of death" has struck, there can never again be an "hour of life." Yet the "hour" of Christ, when it was struck, was at once the hour of death, of victory, of life and of glory. *Father, the hour has come; glorify your Son that your Son may glorify you.*

More important than the eschatological sign of renewed physical life is the sign par excellence: *The gospel is preached to the poor.* This means that the prophetic message of salvation, the fulfillment of the divine promises is now formally announced to the anawim, to those who hungered and thirsted for the kingdom because they had no hope but the Lord. And therefore the last days have come. It is the end, because the fulfillment which earth and time could not give, is now at hand. This fulfillment has begun because now Christ has appeared in the midst of the poor as one of them, and has taken them to himself so that they are, in a most special way, himself. What happens to them happens, in a very particular way, to him.

The Last Days have come not merely because the poor have *heard about* Christ but because they "are" Christ. The poor themselves now become an eschatalogical sign of Christ, a sign by which other men are judged, for *if the wicked servant says in his heart: "My Lord delays in coming" and begins to strike his fellow servants, and eats and drinks with drunkards, the Lord of that servant will come on the day he does not expect and in the hour which he does not know, and will cut him off* (from Man in Christ) and give him his portion with the hypocrites.

(Meditations on the Liturgy, 50-52)

Thomas Merton (1915-1968) was born in France; he was educated in England, became a Catholic in Rome, and found peace with God at the Cistercian abbey of Gethsemani, USA, which he entered three years after his baptism in 1941. His many writings were based on his experience of the monastic life, both in community and, in his last three years, as a hermit. His thought developed from explorations of life itself to a realization of its universal significance in society and its affinities with Eastern monasticism, especially Zen Buddhism. It was this latter interest that led him to Thailand, where he died as the result of an accident.

Fourth Sunday of Advent

Gospel: Matthew 1:18-24   This is how Jesus Christ came to be born. His mother Mary was betrothed to Joseph; but before they came to live together she was found to be with child through the Holy Spirit.

Commentary: K. Rahner   *T*he angel does not merely tell Joseph that Mary has conceived her child through the power of God—though this fact, which Joseph already knew from Mary, is confirmed by the apparition—but has as his principal message: *Take Mary as your wife.* Be a father to this child, heaven is saying, fulfill the duties of a father toward this child which heaven has sent to your bride. Protect, watch over, love, shield, take care of this child. This duty is laid on Joseph by God himself. We can say, therefore, that he is the foster-father and guardian of the child, not just because his wedded bride has conceived a child from heaven, but because God himself wished him to take the place of a father to the Son of God who has come to save the world.

This is why Joseph is told to give a name to the child; this is why Joseph is addressed as *Son of David* since Jesus himself will be known and acknowledged as the son of David precisely because his earthly father is a son of David stemming from that royal lineage. Thus from our reading of this text we can see heaven entrusting to the care of Joseph the savior of the world. Through this message from above Joseph is drawn into the great, public, official story of salvation. He acts no longer in the purely private capacity of bridegroom and later husband of Mary, but plays an official role in the salvation story. He is the guardian and protector of the Son of God, directly appointed to that office, and not just drifting into this relationship with the divine child through the accident of his betrothal to Mary.

We too are often called to be guardians of the Holy One in ourselves, in our lives, in our work. At first sight, our everyday affairs may seem to have nothing to do with the history of the kingdom of

God and the salvation of the world. We may seem to be concerned with nothing more than the tissue of relationships that makes up our lives, our friendships, our work. But even here we are being called upon to be the guardians of something holy, something great, God's grace in us and about us. Is there anyone who has not some of God's children entrusted to his care: in the home, in the school, in the neighborhood? For us no angel from heaven appears, no dream apparition bids us: Take the child to yourself. And yet it seems as though through purely earthly incidents we are made responsible for what is heavenly and divine, for God's grace in our own hearts and in our earthly surroundings. In all these the Son of God who became man continues his life, and we are all asked whether the task of guarding this Son of God whom we meet in others will find us as true as Joseph, of whom it is said: he was faithful, he took the child and his mother to himself, he spent his whole life guarding the child so that it might become in truth the savior and the life of the world.

(*Biblical Homilies*, 11-12)

Karl Rahner (1901-1984), a Swabian by birth, entered the Society of Jesus in 1922 and was ordained ten years later. After completing his studies at Freiburg and Innsbruck he was appointed to the theological faculty of Innsbruck in 1936. In 1949 he became a professor of dogmatic theology and in 1964 was appointed to a professorship in Munich. As a theological editor his name is associated with Denziger's *Enchiridion Symbolorum* and also with the *Lexikon für Theologie und Kirche* and *Sacramentum Mundi*. He was a peritus at Vatican II and the many volumes of *Theological Investigations* testify to his tireless labor as a theologian. Etienne Gilson drew attention to Rahner's "combination of intellectual modesty and audacity." A theologian of penetrating insight, he was also without doubt a man of God.

Christmas

Gospel: John 1:1-18

In the beginning was the Word; and the Word was in God's presence, and the Word was God.

Commentary: E. Stein

God has come to redeem us, to unite us to himself and to each other, to conform our will to his. He knows our nature. He reckons with it, and has therefore given us every help necessary to reach our goal.

The divine child has become a teacher and has told us what to do. In order to penetrate a whole human life with the divine life it is not enough to kneel once a year before the crib and let ourselves be captivated by the charm of the holy night. To achieve this, we must be in daily contact with God, listening to the words he has spoken and which have been transmitted to us, and obeying them. We must, above all, pray as the Savior himself has taught us so insistently. *Ask and it shall be given you.* This is the certain promise of being heard. And if we pray every day with all our heart: "Lord, thy will be done," we may well trust that we shall not fail to do God's will even when we no longer have subjective certainty.

Christ has not left us orphans. He has sent his Spirit, who teaches us all truth. He has founded his Church which is guided by his Spirit, and has ordained in it his representatives by whose mouth his Spirit speaks to us in human words. In his Church he has united the faithful into one community and wants them to support each other. Thus we are not alone, and if the confidence in our own understanding and even in our own prayer fails us, the power of obedience and intercession will assist us.

And the word was made flesh. This became reality in the stable of Bethlehem. But it has also been fulfilled in another form. *He who eats my flesh and drinks my blood has eternal life.* The Savior, knowing that we are and remain people who have daily to struggle with our weaknesses, aids our humanity in a manner truly divine. Just as our

24

earthly body needs its daily bread, so the divine life in us must be constantly fed. *This is the living bread that came down from heaven.* If we make it truly our daily bread, the mystery of Christmas, the incarnation of the Word, will daily be re-enacted in us. And this, it seems, is the surest way to remain in constant union with God, and to grow every day more securely and more deeply into the mystical Body of Christ.

The Christian mysteries are an indivisible whole. If we become immersed in one, we are led to all the others. Thus the way from Bethlehem leads inevitably to Golgotha, from the crib to the cross. The way of the incarnate Son of God leads through the cross and passion to the glory of the resurrection. In his company the way of every one of us, indeed of all the human race, leads through suffering and death to this same glorious goal.

("The Mystery of Christmas," *Writings of Edith Stein*, 28-31)

Edith Stein (1891-1942), born at Breslau, Germany, of Jewish parentage, studied at Göttingen and at Freiburg im Breisgau under Husserl, the leading phenomenologist. She was received into the Catholic Church in 1922, and in the following year entered the Carmelite convent in Cologne where she received the name Sister Teresa Benedicta of the Cross. At the end of 1938 she moved to the convent at Echt on account of the Nazi persecution of the Jews, but during the German occupation of Holland she was arrested, transported to Poland, and killed at Auschwitz. She was beatified by Pope John Paul II in 1987. Her writings include *The Mystery of Christmas, Eternal Infinite Being, The Science of the Cross*, and *Hymns to the Church.*

Holy Family

Gospel: Matthew 2:13-15.19-23 After the wise men had left, the angel of the Lord appeared to Joseph in a dream and said, "Get up, take the child and his mother with you, and escape into Egypt, and stay there until I tell you, because Herod intends to search for the child and do away with him."

Commentary: Paul VI

As holy scripture teaches us, before it is a sacrament marriage is a great earthly reality: *God created man in his own image; he created him in the image of God: he created them man and woman.* We always have to go back to that first page of the Bible if we want to understand what a human couple, a family, really is and what it ought to be. Psychological analyses, psychoanalytical research, sociological surveys, and philosophical reflection may of course have a contribution to make with the light they shed on human sexuality and love; but they would blind us if they neglected this fundamental teaching which was given to us at the very beginning: the duality of the sexes was decreed by God, so that together man and woman might be the image of God and, like him, the source of life: *Be fruitful and increase, fill the earth and subdue it.* Attentive reading of the prophets, the wisdom books, and the New Testament, moreover, shows us the significance of this basic reality, and teaches us not to reduce it to physical desire and genital activity, but to discover in it the complementary nature of the values of man and woman, the greatness and the weaknesses of conjugal love, its fruitfulness and its opening on to the mystery of God's design for love.

The Christian knows that human love is good by its very origin; and if, like everything else in us, it is wounded and deformed by sin, it finds its salvation and redemption in Christ. Besides, isn't this the lesson that twenty centuries of Christian history have taught us? How many couples have found the way to holiness in their conjugal life, in that community of life which is the only one to be founded on a sacrament!

Love one another, as I have loved you. The ways in which they express their affection are, for Christian husband and wife, full of the love which they draw from the heart of God. And if its human source threatens to dry up, its divine source is as inexhaustible as the unfathomable depths of God's affection. That shows us the intimacy, strength, and richness of the communion which conjugal love aims at. It is an inward and spiritual reality, transforming the community of life of husband and wife into what might be called, in accordance with the teaching authorized by the Council, "the domestic Church," a true "cell of the Church," as John XXIII already called it, a basic cell, a germinal cell in the ecclesial body.

Such is the mystery in which conjugal love takes root, and which illuminates all its expressions. The rapture which moves husband and wife to unite is the carrier of life, and enables God to give himself children. On becoming parents, the husband and wife discover with a sense of wonder, at the baptismal font, that their child is from now on a child of God, *reborn from water and the Spirit*; and that the child is entrusted to them so that they may watch over its physical and moral growth, certainly, but also the opening out and blossoming in him of *the new nature*. Such a child is no longer just what they see, but just as much what they believe, "an infinity of mystery and love which would dazzle us if we saw it face to face" (Emmanuel Mounier). Therefore upbringing becomes true service of Christ, according to his own saying: *Whatever you do for one of these little ones, you do for me.*

(Writings of Paul VI)

Paul VI (1897-1978), born Giovanni Battista Montini, was ordained a priest in 1920 and in 1925 entered the Vatican Secretariat of State. In this service of the Church he filled several important posts until he was named archbishop of Milan by Pius XII on 1 November 1954. Montini was made a cardinal in December 1958, and elected pope on 21 June 1963. During his long pontificate he showed himself to be an intrepid pastor and a determined promoter of the decrees of the Second Vatican Council. In spite of opposition he firmly held the bark of Peter on its course into a new age.

Mary, Mother of God

Gospel: Luke 2:16-21

The shepherds hurried away to Bethlehem and found Mary and Joseph, and the baby lying in a manger.

Commentary: A. Vonier

*L*et us always bear in mind the great truth that the Blessed Virgin's maternity was a most natural maternity in the sense that she fully responded to it, was not overwhelmed by it, that there was no separation between her and her offspring; Christ came from her as her own dear child, the fruit of her own blessed womb. I am right, therefore, in asserting that Mary's maternal function in the conception of Christ was raised to an incredibly high plane of vitality so as to make her maternity not only an instrumental, but a natural maternity. If Mary's mission had been merely to minister the human element to the Word when he became flesh, her maternity would have been just instrumental; it would have existed only to serve a higher purpose. But Mary's role is more than that; she is permanently the Mother of God; her maternity is not a transient ministration, but an abiding dignity that makes her share with God the Father, in literal truth, the parenthood of Jesus Christ.

A threefold hypothesis may make this point clearer still. We can think of a woman being made a mother by the direct productive act of God; in that case the offspring of that mother would not be divine, but human. Then there can be the conception in a woman's womb of a divine person, as happened in the incarnation, but the woman being merely instrumental to the production of the body; in such a case it would be divine maternity in the most restricted physiological sense. Thirdly, there is the glorious possibility of perfect divine maternity with all the graces and privileges, with all the rights and splendors, of one who shares to the full, with God the Father, the parenthood of the God Incarnate. Such is Mary's maternity; such is the meaning of Elizabeth's salutation, or rather the salutation of the Holy Spirit through the mouth of Elizabeth, when full of the divine Spirit she cried with a loud voice: *Blessed are you among women, and blessed is the fruit of your womb. And whence is this to me, that the Mother of my Lord should come to me?* Elizabeth was the first creature to call Mary "the Mother of God"; she gave us the grandest title of our Lady: "Mother of God." The archangel, indeed, had said as much, but only by implication; Elizabeth, the happiest of human mothers, has the privilege of having spoken for the first time the words "Mother of God." When, moreover, in the same breath she calls blessed the Mother and the fruit of her womb, bestowing the same encomium on the two lives which were not yet disjoined, she gives us an additional reason for saying that Mary's maternity had been raised to the divine plane of dignity and perfection, where one and the same blessedness holds mother and offspring wrapped in a matchless sanctity.

(The Divine Motherhood, 345-346)

Anscar (Martin) Vonier (1875-1938), born in Swabia, entered the abbey at Buckfast in 1889 and was clothed as a novice in 1893, receiving the name Anscar. He did brilliantly at his studies in Rome and was sent back to Sant'Anselmo as a professor in 1905. In the following year he was to have accompanied his abbot to Argentina but their ship was wrecked; Abbot Natter drowned and Dom Anscar was elected abbot in his place. He presided over the immense task of the rebuilding of the abbey church by the monks themselves and was a source of deep spiritual inspiration by both his personality and his books, which include: *The Personality of Christ, The Divine Motherhood, A Key to the Doctrine of the Eucharist, The New and Eternal Covenant,* and *The Spirit and the Bride.*

Second Sunday after Christmas

Gospel: John 1:1-18

In the beginning was the Word; and the Word was in God's presence, and the Word was God. The Word of God became flesh and dwelt among us.

Commentary: J. H. Newman

*T*he Word was made flesh, and dwelt among us. Thus does the favored apostle and evangelist announce to us that sacred mystery, which we this day especially commemorate, the incarnation of the Eternal Word. Thus briefly and simply does he speak as if fearing he should fail in fitting reverence. If any there was who might seem to have permission to indulge in words on this subject, it was the beloved disciple, who had heard and seen, and looked upon, and handled the Word of life; yet, in proportion to the height of his privilege, was his discernment of the infinite distance between him and his creator. Such too was the temper of the holy angels, when the Father *brought in the first-begotten into the world*: they straightway worshiped him. And such was the feeling of awe and love mingled together, which remained for a while in the Church after angels had announced his coming, and evangelists had recorded his sojourn here, and his departure; there was silence as it were for half an hour. Around the Church, indeed, the voices of blasphemy were heard, even as when he hung on the cross; but in the Church there was light and peace, fear, joy, and holy meditation. Lawless doubtings, importunate inquirings, confident reasonings were not. An heartfelt adoration, a practical devotion to the ever-blessed Son, precluded difficulties in faith, and sheltered the Church from the necessity of speaking.

He who had seen the Lord Jesus with a pure mind, attending him from the Lake of Gennesareth to Calvary, and from the sepulcher to Mount Olivet, where he left this scene of his humiliation; he who had been put in charge with his Virgin Mother, and heard from her what she alone could tell of the mystery to which she had ministered; and they who had heard it from his mouth, and those again whom these had taught, the first generations of the Church, needed no explicit declarations concerning his sacred person. Sight and hearing superseded the multitude of words; faith dispensed with the aid of lengthened creeds and confessions. There was silence. *The Word was made flesh*; "I believe in Jesus Christ his only Son our Lord"; sentences such as these conveyed everything.

(*Parochial and Plain Sermons, II*, 26-27)

John Henry Newman (1801-1890) was born in London and brought up in the Church of England. He went up to Trinity College, Oxford, in 1817, became a Fellow of Oriel five years later, was ordained a deacon in 1824 and appointed vicar of Saint Mary's, Oxford, in 1832. The impact of his sermons was tremendous. He was the leading spirit in the Tractarian Movement (1833-1841) and the condemnation of "Tract 90" led to his resignation from Saint Mary's in 1843. Two years later he was received into the Catholic Church. He was ordained in Rome and founded a house of Oratorians in Birmingham. Newman's *Essay on the Development of Christian Doctrine* throws light on his withdrawal of previous objections to Roman Catholicism; his *Apologia* reveals the deepest motives underlying his outward attitudes, and *The Grammar of Assent* clarifies the subjective content of commitment to faith. In 1879 he was made a cardinal and he died at Edgbaston in 1890.

Epiphany

Gospel: Matthew 2:1-12

After Jesus had been born at Bethlehem in Judea during the reign of King Herod, some wise men came to Jerusalem from the east. "Where is the king of the Jews?" they asked.

Commentary: E. Leen

Everybody knows that the call of the Magi typifies the vocation of the Gentiles to the Church of God. But to penetrate more deeply into this mystery and to read therein an experience common to a multitude of souls demand a deeper understanding of God's way of manifesting himself to his creatures, and a keener discernment of his actions in human souls.

God is a hidden God, and must be so for us. He manifests himself obscurely. God does not hide himself from us purposely or to make approach to him more difficult. He desires revelation of himself to us, and approach to him on our part. God in his approach to us but tempers his brilliancy to accommodate it to our weak and diseased spiritual vision. He, as it were, takes care not to hurt our soul's sight. But he aims at revelation through dimmed radiance. The incarnation, which is the utmost concealment of the Godhead that there is, or that can be—except that of the eucharist alone—is the greatest revelation of God.

That we are dull of perception is certainly not due to the mode in which God reveals himself, but must be traceable to our fault. It is the poor quality of our faith that is responsible for this dullness. We do not take God on his own conditions. We are always given to imposing ours on him. We have a tendency to decide for ourselves what shall be the sensible exterior vesture of God's message. We clothe that message with a garment woven of our own ideas and imaginings, and we reject the material selected by God himself for his revelation.

Not so the wise men. They took God on his own terms. We choose a certain mode for his manifestation, and they acknowledged him as God in the lowliness of the guise in which he appeared. They looked on a babe and they said God. Their faith was superb.

32

That the three wise men were able to discern in the form of a helpless babe, lying in an earthly Mother's frail arms, under a miserable roof, the king of kings, the great redeemer of the human race that had been spoken of in prophecy for centuries before, was a truly marvelous thing. It is a proof that they must have been men of very pure lives and to a large extent immune from the corruption of the world in which they lived. Gifted with great science, as their name implies, they must have had clear and docile and simple minds, minds eager to acquire the truth and ready to submit to it, no matter how much it might conflict with the traditions and prejudices of their race.

The wonderful faith of these men passes all belief. Their appearance in the pages of Saint Matthew is like a sudden burst of glorious sunshine, breaking in a flood of glory, through a sky wrapped in a mantle of somber grey. *And the star went before them, until it came and stood over where the child was; and seeing the star they rejoiced with exceeding great joy. And entering into the house they found the child with Mary his Mother.*

Their long quest had come to an end. As they saw the humble roof under which the child was, and as they perceived the lowly simple condition of his parents, were they taken aback? Had they any misgivings? Were they harassed by any doubts? Were they expected to discern in this humble babe an object of their kingly homage? It was the supreme test to which they were put, and their magnificent faith triumphed over all appearances. Their hearts responded loyally to the touch of grace, for they were unprejudiced and ready to concede to God whatever form he should choose for his manifestation.

(*In the Likeness of Christ*, 56-68)

Edward Leen (1885-1944) was born at Abbeyfeale, Ireland, and educated at Rockwell College, Cashel. In 1909 he made his profession in the Congregation of the Holy Ghost at Chevilly, France. After having acquired a doctorate in theology in Rome, he was sent to Nigeria as a missionary and then returned to Dublin after two years as dean of studies and subsequently president of Blackrock College. He wrote several books in the line of Columba Marmion's spirituality; he was also influenced by Francis Libermann, C.S.Sp.

Baptism of the Lord

Gospel: Matthew 3:13-17   Jesus came from Galilee to the Jordan to be baptized by John.

Commentary: F. X. Durrwell   The theophany of the Jordan marks the beginning of Christ's public life. God guarantees Jesus of Nazareth: the voice from heaven shows that he is the Son; the presence of the Holy Spirit shows that he is the Messiah, the Anointed One of Yahweh, upon whom the power of God rests. Like the heroes of old, Christ enters upon his career by the impetus of the Holy Spirit. This is the meaning of the theophany; but the baptism of our Lord, taken as a whole, has a larger and more complex significance.

John was the herald going ahead to open the road, the friend leading the way. The demand he must fulfill was preparing the road, and ushering in his greater friend. The demand Christ must fulfill was to be the savior of the sinful people. The meeting between them brought John to the culminating point of his mission as he, as it were, ushered Christ into his work of redemption. And Christ entered upon that work. The baptism was the prelude to the redemption, and there lies the mystery of it.

It was a prelude in symbol as well as in reality, for the whole act of redemption was reflected in it and begun in it. Our Lord must place himself among sinners and submit to *baptism unto penance.* He was later to submit to another baptism: *I have a baptism wherewith I am to be baptized. Can you be baptized with the baptism wherewith I am to be baptized?* His immersion in the water of penance was an anticipation and a figure of the blood and suffering of that other baptism. Corresponding to that momentary humiliation there was a glorification: *And Jesus, being baptized, forthwith came up out of the water; and lo, the heavens were opened to him: and he saw the Spirit of God descending as a dove, and coming upon him. And behold a voice from heaven saying: This is my beloved Son, in whom I am well pleased.* Jesus came up out of the Jordan as later he was to rise from the dead, in the glory of the

Spirit, in the manifestation of the divine sonship; the new creation which was to be fulfilled in the resurrection was already promised.

The baptism of water to which Christ had to submit himself was, therefore, related to his essential work of death and resurrection: it was as it were a preliminary sketch of the work of redemption. From then onward, John the Baptist, who had not known him before except as a judge to be feared, called him *the Lamb of God who takes away the sin of the world*. It is also significant that this anticipation of the drama of the redemption took place in a ritual of water: Christ was rehearsing for his death and resurrection by entering the waters of baptism and emerging from them.

Thus the baptismal teaching of the synoptics offers many suggestions. Christian baptism is linked with the tremendous promises of the prophets and of John the Baptist, and with that eschatological baptism in the Spirit out of which the messianic people are to be born. Only later was theology to relate this outpouring of the Spirit to the glorification of Christ. But the account of his baptism even as it stands brings to mind the whole drama of the redemption, and enables Christians to see the sacrament of water as an extending to them of the great eschatological event of our Lord's death and resurrection.

(*The Resurrection*, 313-315)

Francis X. Durrwell (1912-   ), a Redemptorist born in Alsace, is characterized by the total honesty with which he views the sacred text. Having chosen to pursue a biblical and historical theology, he does not accommodate the word of God to the exposition of his point of view, but submits his researches to the enlightenment to be attained by scriptural witnesses. He also was superior of his province in Strasbourg and is best known for his work *The Resurrection*.

First Sunday of Lent

Gospel: Matthew 4:1-11   Jesus was led by the Spirit out into the wilderness to be tempted by the devil.

Commentary: J. Bonsirven

Jesus chose to emphasize his solidarity with sinners by undergoing the trial which all created beings have to pass through—the trial of temptation. The reason why the various gospel traditions all record this incident is that they want to mark its predominant importance in the Savior's career. We know about this incident because its hero was willing to give an account of it. Our leader endured it for our sakes so that he could more easily feel for us, as the letter to the Hebrews tells us, in our humiliations. The temptation was not aimed at the three forms of concupiscence, from which Christ was exempt. It sets out, in the form of a parable in action, the crucial choice which faced the Messiah at the outset of his career: the choice between the conception of the prophets and providence on the one hand and that formed by many of the Jews on the other. The divine point of view and the human—the one which the adversary of the kingdom of God had to maintain. Here again he intervenes, not as the personification of an abstract idea, but as a real individual. His promptings appear to be directed only to the intelligence, but surely, as in the agony of Gethsemani, our Lord's feelings were also affected. If we admit that Christ really acquired knowledge by experience, we must conclude in the words of the letter to the Hebrews that he *learned obedience in the school of suffering*. Hence, it was a real and thoroughgoing temptation, "only sinless." And the tempter held out alluring prospects which should have been irresistible. Making use of biblical texts, he painted a glowing picture of the assured success of a divine mission.

Let the Son of God use his power to appear as the expected Messiah, dispensing manna to the people like Moses. Let him appear, not riding on an ass, but descending from the clouds, the Lord and Ruler of all things. To these promptings, Jesus replied by the profession of the principles which must serve every child of God as a guide to conduct: divine injunctions come before material benefits. It is wicked to try to impose one's own will on God. Power, sought for its own sake, cannot be gained without entering into a pact with Satan, without misunderstanding one's first duty, which is to worship God and serve him alone.

This rebuff did not discourage the adversary. He left him, but only for a while. He returned to the attack through the intermediary of the Pharisees and the other masters of Judaism. Especially was he to come to the fore at the moment of the passion, which was his work, principally in the agony of Gethsemane, the supreme temptation. Here again, Christ's unconditional obedience to his Father's commandments led him to offer the perfect and decisive sacrifice and thus complete the defeat of Satan.

(*Theology of the New Testament*, 55-56)

Joseph **Bonsirven** (1880-1958), after his education and ordination at the Sulpician seminary in Paris, was assigned to teach scripture at the major seminary of Albi. In 1906 he studied at the École Biblique under Père Lagrange; in 1909 he received his licentiate in sacred scripture from the Pontifical Biblical Commission. The following year his doctoral thesis on rabbinic eschatology was not accepted, and he was forbidden to teach scripture. Bonsirven humbly accepted the decision and returned to his diocese for pastoral work, which was interrupted by service and subsequent imprisonment in World War I. While a prisoner of war, he was appointed by Benedict XV to teach dogmatic theology and scripture to imprisoned seminarians. After the war he joined the Society of Jesus and returned to teaching New Testament exegesis in France and then in Rome at the Biblical Institute.

Second Sunday of Lent

Gospel: Matthew 19:1-9

Jesus took with him Peter and James and his brother John and led them up a high mountain where they could be alone. There in their presence he was transfigured.

Commentary: John of the Cross

God has now so spoken, that nothing remains unspoken; for that which he partially revealed to the prophets he has now revealed all in him, giving unto us all, that is, his Son. And, therefore, he who should now inquire of God in the ancient way, seeking visions or revelations, would offend him; because he does not fix his eyes upon Christ alone, disregarding all besides. To such a one the answer of God is: *This is my beloved Son, in whom I am well pleased, hear him.* I have spoken all by my Word, my Son; fix your eyes upon him, for in him I have spoken and revealed all, and you will find in him more than you desire or ask. For if you desire partial visions, revelations, or words, fix your eyes upon him, and you shall find all. He is my whole voice and answer, my whole vision and revelation, which I spoke, answered, made, and revealed, when I have him to be your brother, master, companion, ransom, and reward. I descended upon him with my Spirit on Mount Tabor and said, *This is my beloved Son, in whom I am well pleased, hear him.*

It is not for you now to seek new oracles and responses: for when I spoke in former times it was to promise Christ: and the prayers of those who then inquired of me were prayers for Christ and expectations of his coming, in whom all good was comprehended, according to the teaching of the evangelists and apostles. But, now, he who shall inquire of me in the ancient way, or hope for an answer at my mouth, or that I should make to him any revelation, shows that he is not content with Christ, and therefore grievously wrongs my beloved Son. While you have Christ you have nothing to ask of me, nothing to desire in the way of visions or revelations. Look well unto him, and you will find that I have given all this and much more in Christ. If you desire a word of consolation from my mouth, behold my Son obedient unto me and afflicted for my love, and you will see how great is the answer I give you. If you desire to learn of God secret things, fix your eyes upon Christ, and you will find the profoundest mysteries, the wisdom and marvels of God, hidden in him: *In whom*, says the Apostle, *are hidden all the treasures of wisdom and knowledge*. These treasures will be sweeter and more profitable to you than all those things you desire to know. It was in these that the Apostle gloried when he said, *I judged not myself to know anything among you but Jesus Christ and him crucified*. If you desire other visions and revelations, divine or bodily, look upon his sacred humanity, and you will find there more than can ever enter into your thoughts, *for in him dwells all the fullness of the Godhead corporally*.

(*The Ascent of Mount Carmel II*, 157-158)

John of the Cross (1542-1591), co-founder with Saint Teresa of Jesus of Avila of the Discalced Carmelites, was born at Fontiveros in Old Castille. In 1563 he entered the Carmelite Order at Medina del Campo, and studied at Salamanca before his ordination to the priesthood in 1567. At this time he met Saint Teresa and became an ardent supporter of her movement of reform, for which he suffered greatly. John of the Cross is considered one of the greatest lyric poets of Spanish literature. His mystical teaching rests on his own experience, the study of the scriptures, and the discipline of Thomistic philosophy.

Third Sunday of Lent

Gospel: John 4:5-42

Jesus had come to the Samaritan town called Sychar, near the land that Jacob gave to his son Joseph.

Commentary: C. Marmion

The woman looks at Jesus in astonishment. This poor creature, sunk in the life of sense, grasps nothing of spiritual things. She is more and more astonished; she asks herself how her interlocutor could give her water, having no means of drawing any, and what water could be better than that of this well, whereat the patriarch Jacob came to drink, he and his sons and his cattle. *Are you greater than our father Jacob?* she asks of Christ. Jesus insists upon his reply: *"Whosoever shall drink of the water that I will give shall not thirst for ever. It shall become in him a fountain of water, springing up into life everlasting."* *"Sir, give me this water,"* says the woman.

The Savior then makes her understand that he knows the evil life that she is leading. This sinner, whom grace begins to enlighten, realizes that she is in the presence of One who sees to the depth of the heart: *Are you a prophet?* And immediately her soul, touched by grace, ascends toward the light. She says to him: *Our fathers adored on this mountain: and you say that Jerusalem is the place where we must adore.* As we know, this was a perpetual subject of dispute between the Jews and Samaritans.

Jesus Christ beholds arising in this soul, in the midst of its corruption, a glimmer of good will, enough for him to grant a still greater grace; for as soon as he sees uprightness and sincerity in the search after truth, he brings light; he rejoices to reward this desire for good and justice.

Thus he is about to make a double revelation to this soul. He teaches her that *the hour is here and now is when the true adorers shall adore the Father in spirit and in truth. For the Father also seeks such to adore him.* He manifests himself to her as the Messiah, a revelation that he had not yet made to anyone, not even to his disciples. Is it not remarkable that these two great revelations were made first of all to a poor creature, who had no other title to be the object of such a privilege except her need of salvation and a glimmer of goodwill?

This woman returns justified. She had received grace and faith. She left her water pot and went into the city to preach the Messiah whom she had met. Her first act is to make known *the gift of God*, communicated to her with such liberality.

It is for this end that Jesus spends himself. The Father's will is that Jesus should bring to him the souls that the Father desires to save, that he should show them the way, and reveal to them the truth that leads them to life. That is the whole work of Jesus.

There was nothing in the sinful woman of Sychar to distinguish her from others, unless it was the depth of her misery; but she was drawn to Christ by the Father. Then the Savior receives her, enlightens, sanctifies, transforms her, and makes her his apostle. For *this is the will of the Father who sent me, that of all that he has given me, I should lose nothing; but should raise it up again* to grace here below, while awaiting the last day, when I will raise it up again in glory.

(*Christ in His Mysteries,* 212-213)

Columba (Joseph) Marmion (1858-1923) was born in Dublin and entered the seminary of Clonliffe and completed his studies at Rome, where he was ordained in 1881. He taught philosophy for a time, but on a visit to Maredsous he felt called to the monastic life and took the habit under the name of Columba. He spent several years at Mont-Cesar (Louvain) as prior and professor of theology and was given the post as abbot of Maredsous in 1909, which he held till his death. Dom Marmion was very human and saintly, but demanding in the guidance of souls. The trilogy, *Christ the Life of the Soul, Christ in His Mysteries,* and *Christ the Ideal of the Monk,* published from notes of his conferences, has been very influential among those concerned with the spiritual life. His teaching has the merit of centering spirituality and all ascetical effort on the person of Christ working in us through baptismal grace.

Fourth Sunday of Lent

Gospel: John 9:1-41   As Jesus left the temple, he saw a man who had been blind from birth.

Commentary: A. de Orozco

On hearing what the Pharisees had done to the man born blind, the faithful and merciful Savior sought him out, as Chrysostom declares, and, seeking, found him, as John tells us. He spoke coaxingly to him: *"Do you believe in the Son of God?"* But he said: *"Sir, who is he, that I may believe in him?"* Then Jesus said: *"You have seen him, and it is he who is speaking to you."*

How astonishing and utterly to be praised is the mercy of Christ Jesus! He makes himself known to the sinful Samaritan woman and the blind beggar, but he does not thus open the mystery to the haughty priests and the angry Pharisees. For, O Lord, *you have hidden these things from the wise and the prudent and have revealed them to little ones, for so it pleased the heavenly Father.* O insolent pride, from which the secrets of God are hidden! O splendid and most desirable humility, to which all the mysteries of God lie open! *I am he, who am speaking to you,* says the kindly Teacher. *For my father and my mother have abandoned me, but the Lord has taken me up,* said the prophet. The happy man of whom we are speaking here could have used the same words. Would, my brothers, that parents, friends, and relatives might abandon us, so that Christ might take us in his arms and embrace us! More than that, let all creatures be against us and attack us, provided our King, the creator of the universe, receive us with kindness and show himself to us!

Blessed Augustine says: "Christ now washes the face of this man's mind by putting faith in his heart, so that he might heal the whole person on the sabbath." The man is not ungrateful for so great a blessing, but falls down before Christ Jesus and worships him. Just as the Magi, prostrating themselves, adored Christ as he lay in the manger, and, opening their treasures, gave him gifts with a mystical meaning, all of them being symbols of our holy faith, so this happy

42

man humbly prostrated himself and worshiped Christ as Son of God. As for us, let us fall at Christ's feet and adore and worship him with the utmost awe, so that his grace may illumine the eyes of our mind and, when death comes to us, we may see in his glory, face to face, him whom we now see obscurely, as in a mirror. Honor be to him with the Father and the Holy Spirit through all ages. Amen.

(Sermon 16, Wednesday of the Fourth Week of Lent, 370-371)

Alonso de Orozco (1500-1591) studied at the University of Salamanca before entering the Augustinian novitiate there. His main apostolates in the Order were preaching and writing, and although he was chosen as royal preacher at the Spanish court, he preferred to speak to poor and simple people. His religious life was marked by a spirit of fraternity, gospel simplicity, and moderation in speech. As an ascetic and great mystic, he suffered crisis and spiritual aridity from 1522 to 1551. He was beatified by Pope Leo XIII in 1882.

Fifth Sunday of Lent

Gospel: John 11:1-45

The sisters of Lazarus sent this message to Jesus: "Lord, the man you love is ill." On receiving the message, Jesus said, "This sickness will end not in death but in God's glory, and through it the Son of God will be glorified."

Commentary: J. Saliège

*T*wo days after he receives the message telling him that his friend is sick, Jesus says to his disciples: "Lazarus is dead. For your sakes I am glad I was not there. In any event, let us go to him."

Faith—always faith. The Master demands it, seeks it, and arranges circumstances to make it spring up and grow in souls.

Have confidence, my brothers and sisters, have confidence when our prayers do not seem to be heard. The reason is not that they have not fallen on the heart of Jesus. If the apparent result takes the form of a lamentable fall, the reason is not that he does not see our tears. He follows all the progress of evil with a gaze that nothing can obscure or distract. If he does not come at the hour when you expect him, the reason is that his hour has not yet come.

Alerted to the approach of the Messiah, Martha, always lively and on the move despite her sorrow, comes to meet him. And at the sight of Jesus, she exclaims: *Lord, if you had been here, my brother would never have died.*

The regret that she experiences at the Savior's absence expresses itself in an act of confidence. "If you had been present, you are so good that you would not have let my brother die." And she adds immediately: *Even now, I am sure that God will give you whatever you ask of him.* She does not doubt. Not the slightest shadow of hesitation grazes her soul. Her faith remains entire, absolute, without reservation.

But she does not exhaust all the riches of the heart of Jesus in her hopes. She does not reach the limits of what almighty power can do in the service of goodness. She must grow more in her ambitions, and losing none of her firmness she must become more extended, and without ceasing to be humble she must envisage the miraculous and the impossible. And Jesus is going to lift her up to these heights. For he answers her by a promise whose grandeur surpasses her faith in hope and would seem to disconcert it: *Your brother will rise again.*

Martha is more astonished than gripped. She does not understand. *I know he will rise again,* she replies, *in the resurrection on the last day.* Then Jesus, wishing to make the faith burst out and radiate and command the confidence that he desires to obtain, strips away the veil that hides the secret of his soul: *I am the resurrection and the life: whoever believes in me, though he should die, will come to life; and whoever is alive and believes in me will never die.* And addressing himself to Martha: *Do you believe this?*

Martha's faith awakens; it goes beyond the created, attains the invisible, and grasps the flame of love of the Savior on the very spot where it has taken shape to spread out over the world: *Yes, Lord, I have come to believe that you are the Messiah, the Son of God; he who is to come into the world.*

(Spiritual Writings, 135-136)

Jules Saliège (1876-1956), archbishop and cardinal of Toulouse, from 1928 until his death, lives in the minds of the French people as a great patriot who during the Second World War preferred duty to ease. He also lives in the mind of the Church as the intrepid pastor who was able to unravel contemporary problems and put into practice concrete responses in his diocese which can serve as an inspiration for all. Toward the end of his life, his body was almost entirely paralyzed. Steadfast in trial, he remained with remarkable dynamism at the head of his archdiocese.

Passion Sunday

Palm Sunday

Gospel: Matthew 26:14-27.66 The account of the passion of our Lord Jesus Christ.

Commentary: B. Pascal

Jesus was in a garden, not of delight like the first Adam when he fell and the whole of the human race with him, but in a garden of torture, where he saved himself and the whole of the human race.

He suffered this anguish and abandonment amid the terrors of the night. I believe that Jesus never uttered a complaint except on this one occasion; but this time he did complain because he could no longer contain his anguish: *My soul is sad unto death.*

Jesus sought the companionship and comfort of men. This was unique in his whole life, it seems to me. But he did not receive any because his disciples were asleep.

Jesus will be in agony until the end of the world: we must not sleep during that time.

In the midst of this universal abandonment, when he found the friends whom he had chosen to watch with him asleep, Jesus grew angry over the peril to which they had exposed not him, but themselves; he spoke to them of their own salvation and well-being with gentle affection while they showed such ingratitude, and remarked that *the spirit was willing and the flesh weak.*

When he found them still asleep, untroubled by any consideration either for him or themselves, Jesus showed his goodness by not waking them, and let them sleep on.

Jesus prayed in his uncertainty over the will of the Father, and was afraid of death; but when he knew his Father's will, he went to meet death and offer himself to it: Let us go. Christ came forward.

Jesus prayed to men, and his prayer was not answered.

While his disciples slept, Jesus wrought their salvation. He did it for each of the righteous while they were asleep, and in the void before they were born, and in their sins after they were born.

We implore God's mercy not in order that he will leave us to indulge our vices undisturbed, but so that he will deliver us from them.

If God gave us masters with his own hand, oh how gladly we should obey them! Events are infallibly determined by necessity.

"Be comforted. You would not seek me if you had not already found me."

"I thought of you in my agony. I shed those drops of blood for you."

"Do you want me always to pay with the blood of my humanity without your shedding a single tear?"

"Your conversion is my business; do not be afraid, and pray trustingly as though it were for me."

"I am more of a friend to you than this man or that because I have done more for you than they, and they would not bear what I have borne from you, and would not die for you at the time of your infidelity and cruelty, as I have done, as I am ready to do and do, in my elect and in the blessed sacrament."

(*Pensées*, 335-337)

Blaise Pascal (1623-1662), despite his brief life and incomplete work, was one of the most universal geniuses of modern France and a singularly novel and profound interpreter of the Christian conscience. Pascal's whole life evolved around science, the world, and God.

Easter Triduum

Evening Mass of the Lord's Supper

Gospel: John 13:1-15 It was before the festival of the Passover, and Jesus knew that the hour had come for him to pass from this world to the Father. He had always loved those who were his in the world, but now he showed how perfect his love was.

Commentary: P. Parsch

Maundy Thursday is among the most honored and impressive feasts of the ecclesiastical year. It is the day of Jesus' agony on Mount Olivet, the act which ushers in the sacrifice of redemption. It is the day on which Christ instituted the eucharist, wherein the sacrifice of the cross is perpetuated in the Church and we receive the living bread of heaven to be the nourishment of the life of grace. Moreover, it is the day of the washing of feet.

What does Christ wish to teach by the washing of feet? Obviously we should not be occupied exclusively with the action in itself. Certainly Jesus does not intend to institute a sacrament through this rite, but he wishes to inculcate the dispositions which prompted him to do what he did. These sentiments may be expressed in the three words: love, humility, service. In opposition to the egotism inherited from original sin, Christ sets up the regal virtue of love of neighbor; in opposition to arrogance, also an effect of original sin, he inculcates the virtue of humility; in opposition to lust for power which besets human nature, he teaches us worthy and joyous service of our fellow men. Here in a nutshell we have something that characterizes Christianity—Christianity in all its greatness, but also in its full austerity.

If we want to understand the symbol of the washing of feet, and carry over the lesson into our lives, then we need only look to the life

48

of Jesus. How illustriously the two virtues of humility and love shine forth in his life! And the virtue of charity is the motive of his life: *Greater love no man has than that he lay down his life for his friends.* Loving service of others! This is what characterizes the whole life of our Lord. He did not come on earth to be ministered unto, even though millions of angels desired to serve him. He came to minister unto others, so that by this act of servitude he could offer his life as a ransom for many. And now we behold him kneeling before his apostles, even Judas the traitor, performing the lowly service of washing their feet.

This is Christianity! What more need be said about the matter? Let us, however, put this lesson to profitable use in our lives. It will not suffice to perform an act of loving service only on this day, for example, by inviting an employee or a poor man to eat with us, praiseworthy as this custom may be. No, the lesson derived from the washing of feet must be applied every day, every hour, if I want to be a real Christian. There will be sufficient opportunities to do so. To every man that comes my way, I must be a servant, willing to give him loving service. If Christ was willing to humble himself before Judas and to serve him, may I exclude any human being from my charity?

We must strive to capture the spirit of Maundy Thursday, and to preserve it throughout the year, in fact, throughout life. May the words of our Lord resound in our ears every day: *I have given you an example*, an example of love, an example of humility, an example of the loving service of others.

(*Sermons on the Liturgy*, 140-141)

Pius Parsch (1884-1954) was born in Moravia and became a Canon of Saint Augustine at Klosterneuburg in 1904. After ordination in 1904 he taught pastoral theology and then served as a military chaplain during World War I. Later he concentrated on biblical studies and the connection of the bible and the liturgy. He shared Pius X's concern for bringing the liturgy to the people and making it understood by them. To this purpose he devoted the many editions of liturgical texts and numerous published explanations of the liturgy that made his monastery a liturgical center of Austria, indeed of all the German-speaking lands.

Good Friday

Gospel: John 19:17-30   The account of the passion of our Lord Jesus Christ.

Commentary: P. Arrupe

*I*t was noonday and everything was dark. Also in Christ's heart there was the deepest darkness. All his friends had deserted him. Even the Father with whom the Son is one, to the extent of jointly begetting the Holy Spirit of love, has now left him alone. Such a dereliction, which he had already experienced in the prayer of the Garden, was necessary in God's plan, that we might grasp the meaning of this Fourth Word of Christ, the living Christ of today.

Today some people are under the impression that God is absent from this world of ours. Not only because of the terrible scenes of injustice and violence we have just recalled, but also because of the void existing in many human hearts. It is well known that the clinics of psychiatrists are well patronized by people in search of peace of mind or of happiness never enjoyed.

But we need not go to psychiatric parlors or hospitals; it is enough to visit one of our supermarkets or department stores to get a further proof of the anxiety and greediness with which people devote themselves to the mad chase of our times—the adventure of consumerism. Modern man has created for himself these miniature substitute-gods to fill the vacuum of his heart. And thus he idolizes the motor car, travel and tourism, cinema stars and the heroes of sport and song. Yet, at night, when this man returns to his apartment and removes his coat to go to bed, he feels on his lips the bitter taste of emptiness.

Similarly, the person of today is in search of strong experiences to fill this void. And thus arises another form of consumerism in today's society, which is still more frustrating—the sorry and grotesque idol of erotism. For sexuality, this beautiful dimension which God has given to man, loses its meaning when it is sought for its own sake and not as a vehicle of a great human love. What happens then? You see it every day. The hunger for love and mystery existing within man's heart ventures into insignificant spiritual escapades. Hence arises the present craze for horror spectacles, the horoscopes, magic and witchcraft, the devil, exorcisms, the superficial knowledge of eastern religious practices.

Meanwhile, the vast majority will not question the situation and think only of living from minute to minute and enjoy life as much as possible, with no thought for the meaning of things. With our present enjoyment of life we expect to drug ourselves against our thirst for God.

Jesus, however, in this utter loneliness of his death, does not despair in spite of the sense of rejection which he has accepted for our sake and raises his eyes to the Father. He calls him, as he had done in the garden, when in his anguish he accepted the Father's will.

Today's world too, in the midst of gloom and obscurity, offers signs to men of faith. Despite the false messiahs, we witness a serious concern for human rights. And when a man devotes himself to the disinterested service of his brothers he begins to discover God. We see those who with a great sense of responsibility set out to seek more just structures, share the life of the poor, and struggle for a progress which is not only material.

God is alive and more present than many imagine. The abandonment, the total solitude of Christ on the cross has yielded its fruit. It looks as though our eyes could see only what is negative. But the power of the one crucified has set the earth on fire and the Spirit is doing his work in each man's heart. We must cleanse our sleepy eyes and learn how to see. We shall be surprised and we shall burst into an irrepressible shout of praise.

(Justice with Faith Today, 217-219)

Pedro Arrupe (1907-1993), born in Bilbao, Spain, entered the Jesuits in 1927. He was educated in Spain and in the United States. In 1936 he was ordained to the priesthood. From 1938 to 1965 he served in Japan in various capacities. In 1965 he was elected superior general of the Jesuit Order. Because of a stroke he resigned in 1983. He led his order in difficult times, but he was always gentle and compassionate.

Easter Vigil

Gospel: John 20:1-9

After the Sabbath, as the first day of the week was dawning, Mary Magdalene came with Mary to inspect the tomb. Suddenly there was a mighty earthquake, as the angel of the Lord descended from heaven. He came to the stone, rolled it back, and sat on it.

Commentary: A. de Orozco

Come and joyfully dwell a while in heartfelt contemplation of our abundant redemption. For our King, who could have done away with the sins of the entire world with a minimum of effort, was unwilling to restore us to our original freedom by simply enduring some anxiety or other, some little affliction. Rather he piled up countless toils for himself in every area of life and, beginning with the tears and weeping of the manger, like a splendid giant joyfully ran the way of the passion; he did not turn his back on any suffering but for our salvation chose a bewildering death on a cross, a death so shameful in the eyes of human beings.

Review all these things, beloved, and measure them one by one with the heart's affection; weigh each of them in the light of reason as you ponder them in your hearts; meditate on them with a healthy appreciation so that you may experience their spiritual sweetness as you see what a sweet and meek lamb Jesus Christ became, who loved us with all his heart. He deigned to redeem us not simply with his tears and his hunger and thirst, though he suffered severely from these for our salvation. Rather he shed his very blood, allowed his body to be scourged, his head to be torn and stabbed by thorns, his hands and feet to be pierced by fearsome nails, and, finally, his side to be opened by a cruel spear, and so came even to death for our redemption. How distressing must have been the thirst of this man who so desired eternal life for us that he did not hesitate to abandon his own life to the hands of his enemies.

Fearing, therefore, beloved, that we might forget these great gifts and heedlessly plunge into the depths of ingratitude, Saint Paul rightly strives to exhort us: *You have been bought with a great price; glorify and bear God in your bodies.* It is as if he were saying: Be continuously mindful of your marvelous redemption; meditate on it without ceasing. Be mindful of the marvels he wrought at the Red Sea, as Moses tells us, marvels wherein the passion of Christ was prefigured. By his incalculable power he destroyed all the treacherous Egyptians in hell and all the curses upon us as well; furthermore, in the waters of his blood, he drowned all our sins, not one of which remained that could not be wiped away by this saving medicine. Recall these marvels, beloved, tell each other of these wonders day after day. Stir one another to love of so great a Redeemer; with tireless praises glorify God *who has loved us*, as Saint John says, and washed our sores and the festering scars of our sins not with water drawn from some ordinary fountain of stream but with his own precious blood that surpasses in value all gold and silver and shining gems. Therefore, brothers, *glorify God in your bodies;* make a return to him by ceaselessly thanking him as he deserves and praising Christ Jesus with fervent spirit.

(First Sunday of Advent, Sermon 1: *Opera Omnia I*, 20)

Alonso de Orozco (1500-1591) studied at the University of Salamanca before entering the Augustinian novitiate there. His main apostolates in the Order were preaching and writing, and although he was chosen as royal preacher at the Spanish court, he preferred to speak to poor and simple people. His religious life was marked by a spirit of fraternity, gospel simplicity, and moderation in speech. As an ascetic and great mystic, he suffered crisis and spiritual aridity from 1522 to 1551. He was beatified by Pope Leo XIII in 1882.

Easter Sunday

Gospel: John 20:1-9

Early in the morning on the first day of the week, while it was still dark, Mary Magdalene came to the tomb. She saw that the stone had been moved away, so she ran off to Simon Peter and the other disciple (the one Jesus loved) and told them, "The Lord has been taken from the tomb! We don't know where they have put him!"

Commentary: M. Hellwig

The whole preaching of Jesus concerning the coming reign of God emphasized essential non-violence. The rule of God is not by compulsion, that is by extrinsic sanctions, but rather by sharing of vision and wisdom and purpose, by invitation and patient waiting upon the freedom of those invited. That which constituted the tragedy of the ministry of Jesus, also constituted its most coherent statement, for in response to rejection, Jesus did not resort to violence, not even to subtle violence to people's consciences and freedom. He stood his ground in the witness he personally had to give, as speaking the compassionate and longing word of God into the human situation, and for this he was crucified. But he spoke the compassionate word of God into the world in all the truth of its non-violent respect for the free response of those who were not yet ready to respond. And because of this God raised him from death, giving him a name above every name, a name in which all might be saved from the confusion and frustration of a sinful history under the crushing spell of the fear of death.

It is this many-faceted compassion of Jesus that offers the key to the resurrection. It is a compassion that goes out to every kind of human suffering both in healing and in challenge, a compassion that respects the freedom and patiently invites response from those who are unfree, gently liberating them by affirmation and respect and expectation. But it is also a compassion in a more radical sense in that he enters into the situation of suffering, the situation of their enslavement to sin and fear and frustration. He enters into it all the way to the bitter end, an ever present and most extraordinary companion in the human dilemma and the diabolic trap. He redeems the situation of hopelessness by being there, because where he is is after all not quite hopeless.

This is the power of Jesus, but it is most typically the power of God, though our thinking and imagining has had to be turned upside down by the encounter with Jesus to recognize it. In acting this way Jesus acts divinely, and in acting this way Jesus embodies his own experience of intimacy with God in such a way that in the encounter with him that experience becomes ours. The resurrection of Jesus is above all else the revelation and the realization of God-with-us, and the token of it is that the presence of Jesus has become interior to our consciousness, interior to our freedom, not doing things for us as we remain passive but empowering us.

In the total self-gift of his compassion, Jesus acts most divinely, yet it is in the same compassion that he becomes in his resurrection most imitable. To be a follower of Jesus means in the first place to enter by compassion into his experience, with all that it expresses of the divine and of the human. And it means in the second place to enter with him into the suffering and the hope of all human persons, making common cause with them as he does, and seeking out as he does the places of his predilection among the poor and despised and oppressed. This would seem to be the meaning of eucharist and the meaning of Church.

(Jesus, the Compassion of God, 106-108)

Monika Konrad Hellwig (1929-   ), born in Breslau, Germany, studied at the University of Liverpool and earned her doctorate in 1968 from The Catholic University of America. She has taught in the United States and overseas and is esteemed for her clear explanations of Christian belief.

55

Second Sunday of Easter

Gospel: John 20:19-31

In the evening of the same day, the first day of the week, the doors were closed in the room where the disciples were, for fear of the Jews. Jesus came and stood among them.

Commentary: W. J. Burghardt

What made Thomas so skeptical, so mulish, when trusted friends like Peter, James, and John told him *We have seen the Lord*? We do not know. What we do know is that the doubter uttered the most perfect affirmation of Christ's nature in all the gospels. "Lord and God" translates the name of Israel's name; "Lord and God" would become the common Christian confession of Christ, Son of God equal to the Father.

How did it happen? Easy, you will say; easy as falling off a log. After all, wasn't his Lord and God standing in front of Thomas? Was it not obvious he had risen from the dead? Only a fool would deny the evidence of his eyes.

Not so fast, my friends. Thomas did not "see" God; what he saw was a man. A unique man, I admit, a wonder man in risen flesh who appeared out of nowhere and walked through doors and still wore the wounds of his dying. Nevertheless, all Thomas could see with his eyes, all sheer reason could reveal to him, was a man. Remember when Jesus' friend Lazarus came forth from the tomb in Bethany? Not a single spectator shouted "My Lord and my God!" An infinite gulf separates "You are risen" from "You are God." The cry of Thomas went far beyond the evidence.

Because it exceeded the evidence, "My Lord and my God" was an act of faith; and faith for Thomas, as for us, was a gift, impossible without God's gracious giving. It was a response to God's self-revealing. Not simply the assent of his intellect to what God had certified: "I firmly believe that you are my Lord and my God." Faith is not a narrow head-trip. Faith in its fullness is a response of the whole person—not mind only, but heart and emotions and will as well.

Thomas' cry was a doxology; I mean a paean of praise, of adoration. It was a yes to his Lord, a total gift of himself to his God.

Such faith is an experience. Personal, of course—a one-to-one experience of God. But notice: The experience took place in the midst of a community a-borning, disciples who had journeyed to Jerusalem with Jesus, had shared his supper, had watched him die from near or afar.

Your faith, like Thomas' faith, is a living faith when "My Lord and my God" is the flaming response of your whole being to the risen Jesus present before you, around you, within you; when it means "I love you, Lord, with every fiber of my flesh, every stirring of my spirit." And that, my friends, is an experience of God. Not a vision. Simply, you and God have touched.

(*Grace on Crutches*, 76-78)

Walter J. Burghardt (1914-   ), a member of the Society of Jesus, has been a leading practitioner of homilectics in the English-speaking world. From 1946 to 1978 he was professor at Woodstock College, Maryland and New York. From 1974 to 1978 he also taught at The Catholic University of America; from 1979 to 1980 he was theologian-in-residence at Georgetown University. He is the author of various books.

Third Sunday of Easter

Gospel: Luke 24:13-35

On the first day of the week, two of the disciples were on their way to a village called Emmaus, seven miles from Jerusalem, and they were talking together about all that had happened.

Commentary: J. H. Newman

Now observe what was the nature of Christ's presence in the Church after the resurrection. It was this, that he came and went as he pleased; that material substances, such as the fastened doors, were no impediments to his coming; and that when he was present his disciples did not, as a matter of course, know him. Saint Mark says he appeared to the two disciples who were going into the country, to Emmaus, in another form. Saint Luke, who gives the account more at length, says that while he talked with them their hearts burned within them. And it is worth remarking, that the two disciples do not seem to have been conscious of this at the time, but on looking back they recollected that as having been, which did not strike them while it was. *Did not, they say, our heart burn within us, while he talked with us on the way, and while he opened to us the Scriptures?* But at the time their hearts seemed to have been holden (if we may use the expression) as well as their eyes. They were receiving impressions, but could not realize to themselves that they were receiving them; afterward, however, they became aware of what had been.

Let us observe, too, when it was that their eyes were opened; here we are suddenly introduced to the highest and most solemn ordinance of the gospel, for it was when he consecrated and broke the bread that their eyes were opened. There is evidently a stress laid on this, for presently Saint Luke sums up his account of the gracious occurrence with an allusion to it in particular: *They told what things were done on the way, and how he was known to them in the breaking of bread.*

For so it was ordained, that Christ should not be both seen and known at once; first he was seen, then he was known. Only by faith is he known to be present; he is not recognized by sight. When he opened his disciples' eyes, he at once vanished. He removed his visible presence, and left but a memorial of himself. He vanished from sight that he might be present in a sacrament; and in order to connect his visible presence with his presence invisible, he for one instant manifested himself to their open eyes; manifested himself, if I may so speak, while he passed from his hiding-place of sight without knowledge, to that of knowledge without sight.

(*Parochial and Plain Sermons*, VI, 131-133)

John Henry Newman (1801-1890) was born in London and brought up in the Church of England. He went up to Trinity College, Oxford, in 1817, became a Fellow of Oriel five years later, was ordained a deacon in 1824 and appointed vicar of Saint Mary's, Oxford, in 1832. The impact of his sermons was tremendous. He was the leading spirit in the Tractarian Movement (1833-1841) and the condemnation of "Tract 90" led to his resignation from Saint Mary's in 1843. Two years later he was received into the Catholic Church. He was ordained in Rome and founded a house of Oratorians in Birmingham. Newman's *Essay on the Development Christian Doctrine* throws light on his withdrawal of previous objections to Roman Catholicism; his *Apologia* reveals the deepest motives underlying his outward attitudes, and *The Grammar of Assent* clarifies the subjective content of commitment to faith. In 1879 he was made a cardinal and he died at Edgbaston in 1890.

Fourth Sunday of Easter

Gospel: John 10:1-10

Jesus said: "I tell you most solemnly, anyone who does not enter the sheepfold through the gate, but gets in some other way is a thief and a brigand."

Commentary: T. Aquinas

Jesus says: *I am the good shepherd.* The title of shepherd is obviously fitting for Christ because just as a flock is tended and fed by a shepherd, so the faithful are nourished by Christ with spiritual food and even with his body and blood. But to make a distinction between himself and a bad shepherd or thief, he adds the word "good"—good, because he carries out the duty of a shepherd, just as a good soldier is one who fulfills the duty of a soldier. But immediately before this Christ said that the shepherd entered by the gate and that he himself was the gate; now that he calls himself the shepherd, it follows that he must enter through himself. And indeed he does enter through himself, because he manifests himself and through himself has knowledge of the Father. We, on the other hand, enter through him because it is through him that we attain beatitude.

Note that no one else but himself is the gate because no one else is the true light except by participation, as it says of John the Baptist: *He was not the light but was to bear witness to the light.* Whereas of Christ it says: *He was the true light which enlightens every human being.* In the same way no one calls himself the gate: Christ reserves this for himself alone. To be a shepherd he granted to others, bestowing this on his members; for Peter was a shepherd, and the other apostles were too, as well as all good bishops. *I will give you shepherds after my own heart,* says Jeremiah. Although prelates of the Church who are sons are all shepherds, he expressly says that no one can be a good pastor unless he is united to Christ by charity and becomes a member of the true shepherd.

Charity is the duty of a good shepherd, and so it says *the good shepherd lays down his life for his sheep*. For this is the distinguishing mark between a good shepherd and a bad one: a good shepherd has the good of his flock at heart; a bad one is out for his own advantage. Ezekiel refers to this distinction when he says: *Woe to those shepherds that feed themselves. Is it not flocks that are fed by shepherds?* So whoever uses a flock to feed himself alone is not a good shepherd. A good shepherd, even in a material sense, endures much for the flock he is bent on tending; as Jacob said in Genesis, *Night and day I was consumed by frost and heat*. But because the welfare of a spiritual flock is more important than the physical life of a pastor, when danger threatens the salvation of his flock, every spiritual pastor should be prepared to lay down his life for the good of his flock. And so our Lord says, *The good shepherd lays down his life*—that is his physical life—*for his sheep*. He does so because he is responsible for them and loves them. Christ set us the example for teaching this: *If Christ laid down his life for us, we should lay down our lives for the brethren*.

(*On John X*, 3, 1-2)

Thomas Aquinas (1225-1274) was born at Roccasecca, near Monte Cassino, of which he became an oblate at the age of five. He was educated at Monte Cassino until he was thirteen, when he was sent to Naples. There he was attracted to the ideal of an intellectual apostolate, and in 1244 he entered the newly founded Order of Preachers, despite strong family opposition. From 1245 to 1248 he studied at Paris under the direction of Saint Albert the Great, and became master of theology in 1256. He subsequently taught in Italy, at Anagni, Orvieto, Santo Sabina, Rome, and Viterbo. In 1269 he was recalled to Paris, but three years later returned to Naples to set up a Dominican school, where he continued work on his *Summa Theologiae*. He died on 7 March 1274 at the Cistercian monastery of Fossanuova on his way to the Council of Lyons. Although his philosophy took its shape from Aristotle, at a deeper level Saint Thomas continued to uphold many fundamental Platonist doctrines which he received from Saint Augustine and Dionysius the Areopagite. In theology he gave special attention to the incarnation and the sacraments. In 1264 Urban IV entrusted Saint Thomas with the composition of the office for the new feast of Corpus Christi. The Church has accepted the substance of his teaching and in 1567 he was declared a doctor of the Church by Pius V.

Fifth Sunday of Easter

Gospel: John 14:1-12

Jesus said to his disciples: "Do not let your hearts be troubled. Trust in God still, and trust in me."

Commentary: J. Bossuet

The Father is in the Son, and the Son is in the Father. Let us enter once more with humility and trembling into the depths of the words of Jesus Christ. He tells us all that he is through these words. The same One whom we see with the eyes of the body, and who in that way appears as man, is the same One in whom we believe, and whom we see with the eyes of the Spirit as the Son of God, and God himself, the same God as his Father; because, hear, O Israel, the Lord our God is one Lord, perfectly one, unity itself; not another God than his Father.

His Father and he are inseparable: The one is in the Other: the Father in his manner is in the Son; the Son in another manner is in the Father. He who sees the Father, sees the Son; he who sees the Son, sees the Father; we do not separate them in our faith, thus conforming to that which he has said: *You believe in God, believe also in me.*

A little while, and now you shall not see me. That is what he will say to us soon. You will no longer see me with the eyes of the body; but shall we no longer see him with the eyes of the spirit? God forbid. Where then would our faith and our hope be? But is he going in such a way that he will no longer remain with us? Again, God forbid. For where then would we find the truth of these words, which we expect to hear soon, *and we will come to him and make our abode with him.*

He really is going away then, and yet he remains; just as when he descended from the bosom of his Father, and yet remained there. Thus when he returns to the Father, he does not remain less with us. In this way, the Man who disappears is the same as the God who remains; the One whom we see, is the same as the One whom we do not see; and he himself is the same with the Father, in order that we may understand that all belongs to us.

62

In the One whom we see, and who has given himself to us in making himself man, we can possess the One who is eternally with the Father, who is in the Father, in whom the Father is, whom we shall see, whom we shall love, whom we shall possess in his Son.

This is the perfect explanation of these: *I am the way*, as man: as Son of God, *I am*, as is my Father, *the truth and the life*: the same truth, the same life. Behold the mystery. Behold the hope. Behold the faith of Christians: to possess the Son who has made himself visible in order to elevate one's self through him, and find in him the invisible truth of God. How close God is to us! How God is within us through Jesus Christ! Truly he is our Emmanuel: *God with us*! Let us sit at his table; let us eat; let us refresh ourselves. There is our nourishment. There is our life.

(*Selections from Meditations on the Gospel, II*, 98-100)

Jacques Benigne Bossuet (1627-1704), outstanding Churchman and orator, was born at Dijon. As the fifth son of the family he was destined for the Church from an early age and educated at Dijon, Metz, and at the Collège de Navarre in Paris. Saint Vincent de Paul prepared him for his ordination to the priesthood in 1652. Seven years later he took up residence in Paris where his fame as a preacher spread rapidly; his funeral orations evoked especial admiration. In 1669 he was appointed bishop of Condom, and in the following year was entrusted with the education of the Dauphin for whom, among other works, his *Discours sur l'histoire universelle* was written. In 1681 he was transferred to the see of Metz: it was for the religious in his charge that the *Méditations sur l'Evangile* and the *Elevations sur les mystères* were written. Among his voluminous writings 137 sermons have been preserved.

Sixth Sunday of Easter

Gospel: John 14:15-21

Jesus said to his disciples: "If you love me you will keep my commandments."

Commentary: G. Vann

The word *paracletos* means first of all a legal assistant, an advocate, a defending counsel; but it also means he who speaks out prophetically, proclaiming, exhorting, enlightening; and this leads to a third meaning, one who consoles, when the message proclaimed is the message of salvation, of hope and of joy. In the first epistle of Saint John our Lord is referred to as a paraclete or advocate who will plead our cause; and this is implicitly affirmed by Christ himself when he tells the disciples he will send them another paraclete to befriend and defend them. But there is an essential difference between the mode of activity of the Spirit and that of the incarnate Word: the mission of the Spirit is the direct result of the mission of the Son: the lifting up of the Son in death and glory brings about the coming down of the pentecostal wind and fire (and thus the essential pattern of sacrifice is fulfilled; for sacrifice, like morality, is *dialogal* in structure); but the Spirit does not simply continue the work of the Son; his activity is of a different kind precisely because it is the activity of the Spirit, whereas the work of the Son was carried out through his human flesh. So our Lord taught the multitudes, but it was as one man teaching another, through the medium of human speech which is addressed to the ear and thence the brain but may fail to penetrate the depths of the personality, to reach the heart. The Spirit will not teach men what they have never been taught before: he will teach them what they have been taught before but have failed to assimilate so fully as to be possessed by the truth in mind and heart alike. It is the hearts of men that the Spirit instructs; and instructs not by an external voice but by his indwelling presence, by being for them precisely the breath of life.

This knowledge, then, is love-knowledge: not a cold, academic apprehension of truths but an assimilation, an affinity, a living and loving union with the truth who is also goodness and beauty and light and life and love; it is the *initia* of the life which is eternal and at the same time the transfiguring process through which man is refashioned in the likeness of love and thereby attains the joy and the peace of which our Lord now speaks: his joy, which will fill their hearts brimful; his peace, which will keep them always in good heart.

(*The Eagle's Word,* 93-94)

Gerald Vann (1906-1963) was educated by Dominicans and in 1923 entered the Order. He was ordained six years later. His studies took him first to Rome and then to Oxford. He returned to Laxton as a member of a teaching staff and afterward became headmaster and superior of the house. He was a prolific author with a special gift for conveying profound truths in a very readable way to a wide public. He was interested in the moral problem of war, and as early as 1936 founded a Union of Prayer for Peace.

Ascension

Gospel: Matthew 28:16-20   One day the eleven disciples set out for Galilee, to the mountain where Jesus had arranged to meet them. When they saw him they fell down before him, though some hesitated.

Commentary: P. Benoit

When the inspired writings speak of Christ *seated* at the *right hand* of the Father, they are obviously only using anthropomorphic images which have no value except their symbolic reference. Commentators have always recognized this. Similarly, when scripture shows us Christ exalted above all the heavens, it simply means to indicate that he dominates our present cosmos, and it would be useless to try and define Christ's position in relation to the "final sphere." The doctors of scholasticism, still bound to Aristotle's system, could go too far in this direction; yet the greatest of them, a Saint Thomas for example, were able to keep a wise and prudent reserve on this point.

The essential teaching of scripture, which is to be retained by our faith, is that Christ, through his resurrection and ascension, departed from this present world, a world corrupted by sin and destined for destruction, and entered the new world where God reigns as master and where matter is transformed, penetrated, and dominated by the Spirit. It is a world that is real with a physical reality, like Christ's body itself, and which therefore occupies a "place," but a world which exists as yet only as a promise, or rather in its embryo, the single risen body of Christ, and which will be definitively constituted and revealed only at the end of time, when the "new heavens" and the "new earth" are to appear.

While waiting for that day, the glorious body of Christ exists somewhere, real, much more real than our perishable world, because it alone possesses true life, but it is useless to ask "where," just as it is mistaken to imagine it "far away." This new world, where Christ reigns and awaits us, is not far away, it is not outside our world, it transcends it. It is of another order, is distinguished in terms of quality rather than of quantity, and we have access to it through faith and the sacraments, in a contact which is mysterious but more real and more close than any contact with our present world can be.

When we say and believe with the Church that the glorified Christ has ascended to heaven and is seated beside his Father, we mean by this that he has penetrated forever into the new, final, spiritual world, of which he is the first cell, a world which is inaccessible to our senses and our imagination, but which is supremely real, much more real than the everyday world about us. And we believe readily, with the mass of the earliest Christian witnesses, that he inaugurated this new world on the day of his resurrection, when he was rapt from the tomb by the Spirit to be exalted next to the Father.

(Jesus and the Gospel, I, 252-253)

Pierre Benoit (1906-1987), a French Dominican, was director of the Biblical and Archeological School of Jerusalem where he taught the New Testament from 1934. He also served as a peritus to the Second Vatican Council. He is well known for his contribution to the *Jerusalem Bible* and his work on the Dead Sea Scrolls. He was author of numerous books and articles. In all this he placed his scholarly exegetical work at the disposal of a large number of the faithful.

Seventh Sunday of Easter

Gospel: John 17:1-11

Jesus raised his eyes to heaven and said: "Father, the hour has come: glorify your Son so that your Son may glorify you."

Commentary: R. Guardini

The farewell prayer of Jesus opens with an expression of his knowledge that *the hour has come* and the wish that he be glorified with the glory that was his before the world was born. Yet it is the hour of Jesus' death; then his glory must lie in his dying. The glory of God transcends form and measure. It is not only joyful, but terrible as well. That Jesus goes to his death in the purity of his oneness with the Father's will—that is glory. That afterward, he rises again from death in the radiance of resurrection—that is the same glory, and identical with the glory that preceded creation and that will succeed it, for eternity remains the same, before or after.

Obedient to the paternal will, the Son *came unto his own* but they refused to accept him. He spoke the word through sermon and deed, but his message found deaf ears and had to remain in the air. He summoned humankind to share in divine life, in that unspeakable "we" of his sacerdotal prayer, but humankind declined, and the Messenger of love was left standing in immeasurable isolation.

In this desolation Jesus turns to the one place where unity is mightier than division and security than doubt: there where the Father commands and the Son obeys; there where the Son gives of himself, and the Spirit carries it into human hearts; there where the divine we of Father and Son through the Holy Spirit controls all things. Here are Jesus' roots; here is his peace, source of his invulnerable strength and union. From here, the beginning, Jesus departed into the world at his Father's command. Now, in the final hour, the Son tells his Father that he has accomplished the paternal will and glorified him on earth by his obedience.

That Jesus' task *is consummated* must be true, because he says so.

Yet what a spectacle of failure! His word rejected, his message misunderstood, his commands ignored. Nonetheless, the appointed task is accomplished, through obedience to the death—that obedience whose purity counterbalances the sins of a world. That Jesus delivered his message is what counts—not the world's reaction; and once proclaimed, that message can never be silenced, but will knock on people's hearts to the last day. Once introduced, the eternal kingdom, too, remains *forever at hand*, ready to enter into time wherever faith opens a door, for Christ is *the way, and the truth, and the life.* Jesus' coming changed the world. From now on it is and will remain the world in which Christ stands. Through this accomplishment the Father has been glorified.

(*The Lord,* 376-378)

Romano Guardini (1885-1968), born at Verona in Italy, grew up in Mainz and was ordained in 1910. Ten years later he was admitted to the faculty of divinity at Bonn. In 1923 he became professor of dogmatic theology at Breslau and in 1945 professor of philosophy at Tübingen. His books were widely read by the laity and had great influence especially on the younger generation. They include: *The Lord, The Faith and Modern Man, The Living God,* and *Sacred Signs.*

Pentecost Sunday

Gospel: John 20:19-23

In the evening of the same day, the first day of the week, the doors were closed in the room where the disciples were, for fear of the Jews. Jesus came and stood among them.

Commentary: O. Casel

*T*oday we celebrate the glorious ending of the great festal season and at the same time its richest unfolding, a sacred mystery in itself. When our Lord Jesus Christ, God and man, died and rose again, God's plan of salvation was fulfilled. The eternal mystery, the plan of salvation which had existed from eternity, was now reality. Sin was expiated, and the barrier between God and the human race was removed.

In Christ the Trinity and the human race meet. Redeemed humanity can speak the same words to the Father as those uttered by the risen Christ: *I have risen and am now with you.* Christ was sanctified and consecrated so that we too might be sanctified in truth. The light of the Holy Spirit has now completely irradiated him; *put to death in the body, he has been raised to life in the spirit.* Even his sacred humanity, which is precisely what makes him our Redeemer, has become wholly spiritual and transfigured. And as Redeemer he is head of the Church which through him is also transfigured and made spiritual. "Where the Spirit of God is, there the Church is," says Saint Irenaeus, "and where the Church is, there is the Spirit of God." When the Spirit of God comes to us, Christ comes to us too. Through the Spirit Christ himself is among us.

All Christians are meant to become like the Son of God. He is indeed the firstborn among many brothers and sisters. We must be filled with the Spirit of God, but it is through the grace of participation, not through hypostatic union that we do so. In this way our soul is transformed supernaturally into the likeness of the Son of God. It is a rebirth. Whoever fails to undergo this regeneration can never see the kingdom of God.

And so at Whitsun we do not honor the third person of the Godhead apart from the other two; we honor the threefold God who sanctifies and divinizes the Church through the gift of the Holy Spirit dwelling in the Church and in every soul. *We shall dwell in their hearts,* Jesus said. We celebrate the completion of the work of our redemption: God as gift, the wonderful messianic gift from above. The Spirit is the gift of God and of Christ to the Church, through which it becomes the bride of Christ and reigns with the holy Trinity. And all this is the result of the cross.

The more we let the Spirit guide us, the greater the power of God's eternal life to grow in us and the nearer we draw to full possession of the Holy Spirit, whom we already see in our risen and glorified Lord Jesus Christ.

(Das Christliche Festmysterium, 76-83)

Odo Casel (1886-1948), a Benedictine monk of Maria-Laach, placed his vast erudition and a veritable passion for research at the service of the liturgy. He set forth in innumerable works his "mystery-oriented" concept of Christian worship. Since his death his teaching has elicited enthusiasm as well as contestation.

Trinity Sunday

Gospel: John 3:16-18

Jesus said to Nicodemus: God loved the world so much that he gave his only Son, so that everyone who believes in him may not be lost but may have eternal life.

Commentary: F. X. McGowan

We owe the Blessed Trinity the homage of grateful love. When we were nothing, the Triune God infused into our common clay a soul made to his image and likeness. What do we not owe the Almighty Father, who has given us life and preserved us, who has provided for our wants and even guaranteed us our pleasures? No one loves like a father, none so compassionate as he; yet as Tertullian says, "No one is so much a Father as the Almighty Father." What do we not owe the Beloved Son, who came from his throne of glory to abase himself to our lowly state, to live a life of persecution and suffering, and to die a slave's death that we might recover heaven? His was the greatest sacrifice the world had ever seen. What do we not owe the Holy Spirit, who enlightened us when we were blind, who upheld us when we were weak, who encouraged us when we were timid, who brought us back to the fold when we had strayed from it, and who forgave us when we had sinned? Everywhere his solicitude has followed us, everywhere his voice has appealed to us. Verily he has been our truest, most faithful, and loving friend. We recall in thought the day of our baptism, when we were carried helpless to the sacred font. Sponsors voiced the vows that were to be the guiding principles of our life; the saving water effaced the stain of sin, and the grace of God restored the image of the divinity disfigured by Adam's fault.

What happiness was breathed into our souls! The Father adopted each one of us as his child, the Son embraced us as his brother, and the Holy Spirit chose us for his temple. Could the Triune God have done more for us? And when in later days we lost our baptismal innocence and lost again our happy privileges, did not the Father, in

72

his mercy, apply the blood of his Son's atonement to our sinful souls, and the Holy Spirit move us to sorrow and repentance? Yes, we have abundant reason to be thankful to the Holy Trinity for its love and mercy toward us; we have forcible reason to love and honor the ever-blessed Three and to offer them the best homage and sincerest worship of our lowly hearts. Well may we repeat the prophet's praise, *Let all the earth adore you, and sing to you: let us sing a psalm to your name.*

(*A Year's Sermons*, 219)

Francis X. McGowan (1854-1903), an Augustinian friar, taught at Villanova University and then served in several Augustinian parishes on the east coast. He was an author of books and articles and he was regarded as one of the most outstanding preachers of his day. He died in Philadelphia at the age of forty-nine.

Corpus Christi

Gospel: John 6:51-59   Jesus said to the crowds of the Jews: "I am the living bread which has come down from heaven. Anyone who eats this bread will live for ever."

Commentary: Y. Congar   *T*he eucharist is the sacrament of the redemptive mystery of the cross which it symbolizes, celebrates, and makes present. It is, in addition, the sacrament of the unity of the mystical body, which it is its special grace to bring into being.

In the eucharist we receive Christ in the form of food. In consequence, according to the law of the sacraments, whose special effects result from what they signify, we unite ourselves to Christ in a mysterious union similar to that obtaining between a living being and its food. In the natural order, the living thing assimilates its food and incorporates it into its own substance. Here, however, the roles are reversed but the effect is mysteriously alike. The eucharist is food and it is certainly our own soul that it feeds with that incorruptible food which is Christ. But whereas, in the natural and material order, all the power of assimilation resides in us so that we reduce what we eat to form part of our own life, here the power of assimilation belongs to Christ and it is he who, in feeding us, unites us and incorporates us with his life. What Truth said to Saint Augustine may be applied to the eucharist: "Eat me and grow in stature. But it is not you who will change me into yourself, like bodily food, it is I who will change you into me" (*Confessions* VII, 10).

The union with Christ which results, an infinitely mysterious one, is like the union which takes place in a living thing; it is both an incorporation and an intensification of life. For, as we have seen, our Lord compares in the most explicit fashion the union he wishes to establish between us and himself, especially through the eucharist, to the unity existing between him and his Father, and that is a unity of perfect life, a substantial unity of life.

The eucharist is, then, the perfect sacrament of our incorporation with Christ. Theologians are unanimous in holding that its special effect is to bring about the unity of the mystical body. By a special increase of grace and of living faith, it incorporates us with Christ precisely inasmuch as it takes us all into the supreme act of love by which he offered himself for us on the cross, *so as to bring together into one all God's children, scattered far and wide.*

We cannot, then, communicate in isolation from our brethren. We communicate in the true body of Christ only by communicating at the same time in his mystical body; the "breaking of bread" brings with it, inseparably, the presence of Christ uniting us to himself and that of the multitude which shares in his redemption—*the one bread makes us one body, though we are many in number.* There we have the whole mystery of the mystical body.

(*The Mystery of the Church*, 132-134)

Yves Congar (1904-   ), a French Dominican, is one of the most respected modern theologians of the Church. He has played a leading role in theological studies, especially in the fields of ecumenism and ecclesiology. He was a peritus at the Second Vatican Council. Father Congar always sought a reform-ist rather than a revolutionary approach to change in the Church, seeking a change that is progressive and desiring to find the answers to present-day situations in the tradition of the Fathers of the Church. He was ordained a cardinal in 1994 by Pope John Paul II.

Sacred Heart

Gospel: Matthew 11:25-30   At that time Jesus said: "Father, Lord of heaven and earth, to you I offer praise; for what you have hidden from the learned and the clever you have revealed to the merest children."

Commentary: Paul VI

*L*et us ask ourselves: how do we picture Christ to ourselves? What characteristic features come to light in the gospel? What does Jesus seem to be like at first sight? Once again, his own words help us. He said, *I am meek and humble of heart.* Jesus wishes to be regarded as such, to be seen in this way. And if we could see him, that is how he would look, even though the vision of him which the Apocalypse presents fills his heavenly form with shape and light. This characteristic of sweetness, goodness, and meekness above all, is essential; and when we think about it we perceive that it both reveals and conceals a fundamental mystery about Christ, the mystery of the incarnation, of the humble God.

Jesus is the good man par excellence; and that is why he descended to the lowest rung of the human ladder. He became a baby, he became poor, he became a sufferer, he became a victim, so that none of his brothers and sisters among humankind might feel he was above or distant from him; he placed himself at the feet of all. He is for all, he belongs to all, and indeed to each of us individually. As Saint Paul says: *He loved me and sacrificed himself for me.*

So it is no wonder that iconography has always tried to express this mildness, this extreme goodness of Christ. Mystical understanding came to contemplate him in the heart; it has made devotion to the Sacred Heart the fiery furnace and symbol of Christian devotion and activity for us moderns, who value feelings and psychology, and are always orientated toward the metaphysics of love.

But now an objection arises—we hear it especially today. Is this picture of Christ who personifies his own preaching, namely, the beatitudes of poverty, meekness, and non-resistance, is this the true picture of Christ? Is he the Christ for us? Where is Christ the Pantocrat, the strong Christ, the King of kings, the Lord of lords? The reforming Christ, the polemical Christ, the Christ of contestation and anathemas? The liberating Christ, the Christ of violence?

When we consider this alleged contradiction between the picture of a Christ, the Good Shepherd, the Christ who was crucified for love, and another picture, of a virile and severe Christ, indignant and pugnacious, we must reflect well, and see how things are in the original evidence of the gospel, the New Testament, authentic and consistent tradition, and in their genuine interpretation. It seems to us that we have a duty to pay honest attention to all this, especially to Christ's complex personality. He was certainly both strong and mild at the same time, just as he was God and man at the same time. We should consider the reforming energy which he brings into this fallen and corrupt world—certainly not political or anarchical reaction.

We should meditate on the real hopes which he offers humanity. We see then that the figure of Christ presents—over and above the charm of this merciful gentleness—an aspect which is grave and strong, formidable, if you like, when dealing with cowardice, hypocrisy, injustice, and cruelty, but never lacking a sovereign aura of love.

Love alone makes him the Savior. Only through the ways of love can we approach him, imitate him, and bring him into our souls and the ever dramatic vicissitudes of human history. Yes, we shall be able to see him who has lived among us, and has shared our earthly lot, in order to bring his gospel of salvation to the world, and to prepare us for this fullness of salvation.

(Address of 27 January 1971)

Paul VI (1897-1978), born Giovanni Battista Montini, was ordained a priest in 1920 and in 1925 entered the Vatican Secretariat of State. In this service of the Church he filled several important posts until he was named archbishop of Milan by Pius XII on 1 November 1954. Montini was made a cardinal in December 1958, and elected pope on 21 June 1963. During his long pontificate he showed himself to be an intrepid pastor and a determined promoter of the decrees of the Second Vatican Council. In spite of opposition he firmly held the bark of Peter on its course into a new age.

Second Sunday in Ordinary Time

Gospel: John 1:29-34

Seeing Jesus coming toward him, John said: "Look, there is the Lamb of God that takes away the sin of the world."

Commentary: J. Daniélou

*I*t is worth noticing that the synoptic gospels only speak of John as "precursor." Saint John's gospel alone portrays him as "witness." This is due partly to the fact that John the Evangelist, former disciple of John the Baptist, preferred to complete rather than to repeat the synoptic tradition; but partly also to the fact that the doctrine of "witness" is one of the most outstanding characteristics of John's gospel.

John the Baptist's testimony to the divinity of Jesus is expressed in a phrase which most certainly dates from the earliest days, since it recurs like a refrain, with slight variations, in all the texts that recall his witness. Matthew has: *The one coming after me is more powerful than I.* In Acts we read: *As John was nearing the end of his course, he said: "I am not what you think I am. No; after me comes one whose sandals I am not worthy to untie."* Finally, in John, the phrase recurs three times. At first the wording is similar to that of Acts: *Among you stands one who is unknown to you, the one who is to come after me, the strap of whose sandal I am not worthy to untie.* In the last two places the phrase occurs in its most complete form: *He who is to come after me takes rank before me, because he existed before me.*

This phrase is important because it bears witness to Jesus in his very relationship to John the Baptist. By it John designates Jesus first of all as the one who comes after him, that is to say, the one whose precursor he is. To indicate that Jesus is the one to come after him means to point to Jesus as the glory of God come down into the desert, that same eschatological presence of God for which John was appointed to prepare the way. That is why the one coming after John ranks before him; his coming has brought to an end John's mission as precursor, and called him instead to witness that the promises are now fulfilled.

The whole impact of John's testimony is the word *Behold*. That is to say, he affirms that the event he has been foretelling has now taken place. But if the one who came after him ranks before him, it is because he existed before him—here lies the whole force of John's witness. He could have been the precursor of some other man greater than himself, but not existing before him. Such a man might be greater than John, but it would be in the same order of greatness. To affirm, however, that the one coming after him existed before him is to assert that this is the very one who sent him, the only one who existed before him, which is the same as saying that he is the Word of God by whom all things were made, now come to his own people. It is to point to Jesus as the one who existed before time began, and will come at the end of time as alpha and omega, the first and the last: first because he is the eternal Son of God, last because he is the eschatological coming of the eternal Son into time, into this world, to seek those who had gone astray.

(*Jean-Baptiste, temoin de l'Agneau,* 109-110.119-120)

Jean Daniélou (1905-1974), born into a privileged family, his father being a politician and his mother an educationalist, did brilliantly at his studies, and in 1929 entered the Society of Jesus. He came under the influence of de Lubac and got to know Teilhard de Chardin. In 1940 he was chaplain to students in Paris and committed to the cause of resistance. Widely ecumenical in his views, he was a peritus at Vatican II under Pope John XXIII, and was made a cardinal by Pope Paul VI. As an author he was at home in many fields of erudition, including scripture, patristics, theology, and spirituality.

Third Sunday in Ordinary Time

Gospel: Matthew 4:12-23

Hearing that John had been arrested Jesus went back to Galilee, and leaving Nazareth he went and settled in Capernaum, a lakeside town on the borders of Zebulun and Naphtali.

Commentary: J.-M. Tillard

When we give careful thought to what the gospel accounts tell us about the men and women who welcomed the word of Jesus and became his disciples before his condemnation and crucifixion, we discover that it was already possible to attach oneself to him in two ways. Neither of these ways is presented as more perfect than the other, although they differ greatly from one another.

First, there is what I would call the usual way of welcoming the good news and wholeheartedly responding to it, but without forsaking one's usual lifestyle on that account. The people concerned stay at home or keep to their trade. They live the gospel in the fulfillment of their daily task. Who would venture to say that Mary, the mother of Jesus, does not love him in the deepest way imaginable or that her everyday life as a woman in an obscure village is not a life of holiness? On what grounds could one maintain that Martha, Mary, and Lazarus are less holy than the sons of Zebedee? The gospels point out that some of these people remained unswervingly faithful to Jesus, whereas Peter and the apostle took to their heels and betrayed him.

But there is also a group that is more mysterious and elusive: the group of those who "follow Jesus" and "are with him" in a special way. They accompany him throughout his apostolic journeys and as disciples, cling to the person in whom they find everything they are looking for. Such devotion is very demanding. For they have to leave everything, to abandon their everyday relations with the world. They forsake their fishing boats, their home, their fields, and their possessions. But they will not be more perfect on that account. Rivalries will spring up among them; one of them will hand Jesus over to his enemies; Peter himself will deny that he belongs to the little band of disciples.

Now *why* do these men—and possibly a few women—attach themselves to Jesus in this way? Certainly not because of a calculated desire to achieve perfection more surely. Nor with the aim of becoming a group of zealous auxiliaries. Rather they were captivated either by the person of Jesus or by his message and they resolved to give themselves to him by radically yielding to the attraction of his Word. They are not saying to themselves: "No sacrifice is too great if it enables me to attain the kingdom preached by Jesus." What they are saying is: "The kingdom disclosed in Jesus is such that it is worthwhile to give oneself wholly to him, even at the price of the greatest sacrifices."

By electing to break away from certain prevalent values, by leaving their home, fishing boat, and family, they show that for them Jesus is *the one thing necessary*, he who suffices to fulfill what the whole life desires and yearns for. It is not words that proclaim that deep conviction, nor even their obedience to a particular code of moral life, but their concrete style of existence, their special way of fitting into society and the world.

In this way they become, among the people of God, those who ostensibly believe in Jesus and publicly declare for him. They are recognized as "keeping company with the Nazarene, Jesus." Through their very existence, they are saying "yes" to what the God of Israel, the God of their people, proposes to them in Jesus.

This is why, nurtured by that conviction, they will go to the length of giving up their lives in order to cry out to all the good news which they themselves have welcomed, and which contact with Jesus has enabled them to understand in part. Their activity in the service of the nations is, so to speak, the splendor, the glory of their adherence to Jesus.

(*A Gospel Path*, 21-23)

Jean-Marie Roger Tillard (1927-   ), born in France, entered the Dominican Order in 1950. After ordination in 1957 he came to Canada in 1959. He was educated at the Angelicum in Rome where he received a doctorate in theology, and then studied at the Saulchoir in Paris. He taught in the faculty of theology at the University of Ottawa and also was visiting professor in many places. He is a consultor for the Vatican Secretariat for Christian Unity.

Fourth Sunday in Ordinary Time

Gospel: Matthew 5:1-12

When Jesus saw the crowds he went up on the mountainside. After he had sat down his disciples gathered around him, and he began to teach them: "Blessed are the poor in spirit; the reign of God is theirs."

Commentary: B. Häring

*W*hen Jesus saw the crowds he went up the hill. There he took his seat and when the disciples had gathered round him he began to address them. Close attention should be given to each word of the introduction since it provides the key to our understanding of the whole sermon on the mount.

One could think that Jesus tried to escape the crowd by going up the mount where his disciples gathered around him, but this would contradict the whole of the gospel and of our faith. Jesus loves the crowd; he came as the Savior of the world; he shed his blood on Calvary for all. When Jesus gathers his disciples around him, his heart goes out to all even if he attends more specially to those who follow him up the hill to the mount of beatitudes. We cannot truly find Christ and dwell with him unless we join him in his love for all people. But for us to join Jesus Christ in his love of people, we must really gather round him, and come to know him intimately as the Emmanuel—God with us. Whoever conceives the main purpose of life to be keeping busy with others will never radiate the joy, goodness, gentleness, and mercy of the Lord. If we wish to make Christ known to all people, we must first know him as his friends did—as listeners, as persons ready to follow him, even if the way sometimes seems arduous.

We can never allow ourselves as Christians to flee from people, but we are allowed and even urged to retreat from the noise, the distractions, and the idols of the marketplace. We can never learn the wonderful gospel of the beatitudes by means of scientific study. In no way do I want to minimize theological research and reflection, but at

82

the very heart of theology and Christian faith is the experience of Christ's nearness. Jesus tells us: *I am the vine; you are the branches. Whoever dwells in me bears much fruit; apart from me you can do nothing.*

Christ proclaims the beatitudes, and shares with us his knowledge of the Father so that our heart may be filled with joy. If we truly abide in his love and rejoice in his nearness, treasuring up his words in our heart and mind, then we shall come to know his love for all people; we too can then become a source of joy for others. But because of our selfishness, we have to remind ourselves from time to time that we cannot be with Christ and rejoice in him unless we turn our eyes to the multitude, as he did when he went up to the mount of beatitudes.

(*The Beatitudes,* 44-45)

Bernard Häring (1912-   ), born in Tuttlingen, Germany, studied theology at the University of Tübingen. He joined the Redemptorist Order and taught in many places throughout the world, principally in Rome at the Alfonsianum and at the Lateran Pontifical University. He is the author of numerous books and articles.

Fifth Sunday in Ordinary Time

Gospel: Matthew 5:13-16 — Jesus said to his disciples: "You are the salt of the earth."

Commentary: J. Mouroux

What is implied in this wonderful thing called charity: a vivid sense of our own condition as redeemed sinners, a victory over the dreadful reactions of wounded pride, a change of heart toward those who offend us—faith, abnegation, faithfulness; in short, conversion, repeated again and again. Forgiveness of sins thus appears in its true light—not as the indifference of the unaware, or the wise calculation of the well-meaning philanthropist, not even as the impulse of a good heart, but as homage, which may be tragic but is always magnificent, paid to our Father who forgives us, and whom we do our best to imitate.

This love of the neighbor means bearing witness. Being a Christian means serving as Christ served, and with Christ. Christ's essential service is the bringing of truth, salvation, joy. Christians must take part in this service, and this they do by bearing witness. There are two images that express one aspect of this Christian function. First, *You are the salt of the earth.* Like salt, Christians act by contact. The power of purity and faithfulness and charity that is in them elevates their life, saves it from egoism, and gradually delivers it up into God's hands; it gives a spiritual savor to all their actions and makes them an agent of purification and preservation.

Then, *You are the light of the world.* Like light, Christians act by presence. The light of faith, which produces every kind of good work, dissipates prejudices, lightens the way, leads to God. It comes and awakens that power of desire and admiration and "graceful" action that slumbers in every Christian soul, and thus, by its mere presence, it causes us to glorify God. This gospel affirmation is complementary to another. We must never act so as to be noticed by human beings,

84

but only to please God. The purer the intention, the deeper the inwardness of our acts, the more direct and detached will be our search for God and his kingdom—and the more our light will shine before all.

For light does not try to be seen: it only has to exist, and then it is bound to shine; the more purely it is itself, the more brilliantly it shines. So for the Christian people: the more they forget themselves for God, the more they become transparent to the divine light, the more they are bound to spread God around them. Purity of intention, and "candle power," are one and the same thing: it is love for the Father that attracts others to the Father and gives glory to God.

(*The Christian Experience*, 105-106)

Jean Mouroux (1901-1973), after studying at Dijon under Gabriel Brunhes, and finding particular inspiration in the works of Thomas Aquinas and Maurice Blondel, was ordained a priest in 1926. Throughout his priestly life he devoted himself to gaining an ever greater understanding of the human capacity for relationship with God. This theme, developed in strongly personalist terms, is seen in his first and arguably greatest work, *Sens Chrétien de l'homme* (1945). The truth in which he placed his faith was the person of Christ, the real communication of God. For most of his life Mouroux was a professor, first of apologetics, then of dogmatic theology, at Flavigny. He attended the Second Vatican Council as a peritus.

Sixth Sunday in Ordinary Time

Gospel: Matthew 5:17-37

Jesus said to his disciples: "Do not think that I have come to abolish the law and the prophets. I have come, not to abolish them, but to fulfill them."

Commentary: C. Lubich

I f you bring your gift to the altar and there recall that your brother or sister has anything against you, leave your gift at the altar, go first to be reconciled with your brother or sister, and then come and offer your gift.

Here we have one of those sayings of Jesus which, if they were properly understood, could initiate in us a real revolution and which, if it were lived by everyone in the world, would assure peace for ever.

Jesus imagines an Israelite making his way to the temple to offer his sacrifice to God. (Today we might think of one of the faithful going to church to assist at Mass.) For an Israelite of Jesus' time the offering of sacrifice represented the most important moment, the high-point of his relationship with God—as, for that matter, participation in the Mass is for the Christian of today. Well then, says Jesus, making use of the language of paradox so as to emphasize the importance of full accord between brothers or sisters in God's sight: if, when you are on the point of offering your sacrifice, you should remember some lack of agreement between you and your neighbor, break off your sacrifice and first go to be reconciled with your neighbor. For the offering of sacrifice—or, for us Christians, participation in the Mass—runs the risk of becoming an act empty of content if it should be carried out in a lack of accord with our brothers or sisters. The first sacrifice that God looks for in us is that we should try hard to be at peace with all.

It seems that, with this exhortation, Jesus' thought does not offer any substantial change with regard to the Old Testament. For the prophets had already anticipated this idea that, to victims offered to him in sacrifice, God prefers love of neighbor, mercy, and compassion toward the weak. When sacrifices have been offered to him by people who oppress the poor he spurns them as an abomination. Instead of being an act of worship they then become an insult made to God.

But the new dimension exists and it lies in this: Jesus states that it must always be we who are the ones to take the initiative so that good harmony should be kept up, so that fraternal communion be maintained. For he does not say: if you remember having offended your brother or sister but, if you remember that your brother or sister has something against you. For him the very fact of remaining indifferent when faced with a disagreement with one's neighbors, even when we ourselves are not the ones responsible for the disagreement, but others, is already a reason for not being acceptable to God, for being spurned by him.

Jesus wants to put us on our guard here not only against the most serious outbursts of hatred but also every expression or attitude indicating a lack of solicitousness or love toward one's brother or sister.

So how are these words to be put into practice? We must try not to be superficial in our relations but search the most intimate recesses of our hearts. Let us act in such a way as to eliminate even a mere indifference or some lack of goodwill or other, any attitude of superiority, of carelessness toward someone.

We usually try to make up for any rudeness, an outburst of impatience, by asking pardon or by a friendly gesture. And if, on occasion, that does not seem possible, what matters will be the radical change of our interior attitude. Instead of an attitude of instinctive rejection of our neighbor an attitude must be introduced of total, full acceptance, of complete acceptance of the other, of limitless mercy, of forgiveness, of sharing, of attention to their needs.

If we act like this we will be able to offer God any gift we like and he will accept and acknowledge it. Our relationship with him will be deepened and we shall attain that union with him which is our happiness both now and to come.

(From Scripture to Life, 33-35)

Chiara Lubich (1920-   ), born in Trent, Italy, is the foundress and president of the Focolare. She is a member of the Pontifical Council of the Laity, and a leading figure in world ecumenism. In 1977 she was awarded the Templeton Prize for the progress of religions and currently she is an honorary president of the World Council of Religions for Peace.

Seventh Sunday in Ordinary Time

Gospel: Matthew 5:38-48

Jesus said to his disciples: "You have learnt how it was said: Eye for eye, and tooth for tooth."

Commentary: Thérèse of Lisieux

The Lord, in the gospel, explains in what his new commandment consists. He says in Matthew: *You have heard that it was said, "You shall love your neighbor and hate your enemy." But I say to you, love your enemies . . . pray for those who persecute you.* No doubt, we don't have any enemies in Carmel, but there are feelings. One feels attracted to this sister, whereas with regard to another, one would make a long detour in order to avoid meeting her. And so, without even knowing it, she becomes the subject of persecution. Well, Jesus is telling me that it is this sister who must be loved, she must be prayed for even though her conduct would lead me to believe that she doesn't love me: *If you love those who love you, what reward will you have? For even sinners love those who love them.* And it isn't enough to love; we must prove it. We are naturally happy to offer a gift to a friend; we love especially to give surprises; however, this is not charity, for sinners do this too. Here is what Jesus teaches me also: "Give to everyone who asks of you, and from the one who takes away your goods, ask no return." Giving to all those who ask is less sweet than offering oneself by the movement of one's own heart; again, when they ask for something politely, it doesn't cost so much to give, but if, unfortunately, they don't use very delicate words, the soul is immediately up in arms if she is not well founded in charity. She finds a thousand reasons to refuse what is asked of her, and it is only after having convinced the asker of her tactlessness that she will finally give what is asked, and then only as a favor; or else she will render a light service which could have been done in one-twentieth of the time that was spent in setting forth her imaginary rights.

Although it is difficult to give to one who asks, it is even more so to allow one to take what belongs to you, without asking it back. O Mother, I say it is difficult; I should have said that this seems difficult, for *the yoke of the Lord is sweet and light.* When one accepts it, one feels its sweetness immediately, and cries out with the Psalmist: *I have run the way of your commandments when you enlarged my heart.* It is only charity which can expand my heart. O Jesus, since this sweet flame consumes it, I run with joy in the way of your new commandment. I want to run in it until that blessed day when, joining the virginal procession, I shall be able to follow you in the heavenly courts, singing your new canticle which must be love.

(Autobiography, 224-226)

Thérèse of Lisieux (1873-1897), surnamed Martin, became a Carmelite of outstanding tenacity, singleness of purpose, and love of God. She was gifted with an intelligence and sensitivity which disposed her to perceive the significance of the smallest everyday happenings. This capacity, purified by suffering, taught her what she called her "Little Way." During her last illness she wrote, under obedience, the story of her life, which together with her prayer and the quality of her life has brought millions to God. She is a patron saint of missions.

Eighth Sunday in Ordinary Time

Gospel: Matthew 6:24-34

Jesus said to his disciples: "No one can be the slave of two masters: he will either hate the first and love the second, or treat the first with respect and the second with scorn."

Commentary: J. H. Newman

God beholds you individually, whoever you are. He *calls you by name*. He sees you and understands you, as he made you. He knows what is in you, all your own peculiar feelings and thoughts, your dispositions and likings, your strength and your weakness. He views you in your day of rejoicing and your day of sorrow. He sympathizes in your hopes and in your temptations. He interests himself in all your anxieties and remembrances, all the risings and fallings of your spirit. He has numbered the very hairs of your head and the cubits of your stature. He compasses you round and bears you in his arms; he takes you up and sets you down. He notes your very countenance, whether smiling or in tears, whether healthful or sickly. He looks tenderly upon your hands and your feet; he hears your voice, the beating of your heart, and your very breathing.

You do not love yourself better than he loves you. You cannot shrink from pain more than he dislikes your bearing it; and if he puts it on you, it is as you will put it on yourself, if you are wise, for a greater good afterward.

You are not only his creature (though for the very sparrows he has a care, and pitied the *much cattle* of Nineveh), you are a man redeemed and sanctified, his adopted son, favored with a portion of that glory and blessedness which flows from him everlastingly unto the Only-begotten. You were chosen to be his, even above your fellows who dwell in the east and south. You were one of those for whom Christ offered up his last prayer, and sealed it with his precious blood. What a thought is this, a thought almost too great for our faith! Scarce can we refrain from acting Sarah's part when we bring it before us, so as to *laugh* from amazement and perplexity.

What is man, what are we, what am I, that the Son of God should be so mindful of me? What am I, that he should have raised me from almost a devil's nature to that of an angel's, that he should have changed my soul's original constitution, new-made me, who from my youth up have been a transgressor, and should himself dwell personally in this very heart of mine, making me his temple? What am I, that God the Holy Spirit should enter into me, and draw up my thoughts heavenward *with sighs too deep for words*?

These are the meditations which come upon the Christian to console him, while he is with Christ upon the holy mount. And, when he descends to his daily duties, they are still his inward strength, though he is not allowed to tell the vision to those around him. They make his countenance to shine, make him cheerful, collected, serene, and firm in the midst of all temptation, persecution, or bereavement.

(*Plain and Parochial Sermons, III*, 124-126)

John Henry Newman (1801-1890) was born in London and brought up in the Church of England. He went up to Trinity College, Oxford, in 1817, became a Fellow of Oriel five years later, was ordained a deacon in 1824 and appointed vicar of Saint Mary's, Oxford, in 1832. The impact of his sermons was tremendous. He was the leading spirit in the Tractarian Movement (1833-1841) and the condemnation of "Tract 90" led to his resignation from Saint Mary's in 1843. Two years later he was received into the Catholic Church. He was ordained in Rome and founded a house of Oratorians in Birmingham. Newman's *Essay on the Development Christian Doctrine* throws light on his withdrawal of previous objections to Roman Catholicism; his *Apologia* reveals the deepest motives underlying his outward attitudes, and *The Grammar of Assent* clarifies the subjective content of commitment to faith. In 1879 he was made a cardinal and he died at Edgbaston in 1890.

Ninth Sunday in Ordinary Time

Gospel: Matthew 7:21-27

Jesus said to his disciples: "It is not those who say to me, 'Lord, Lord,' who will enter the kingdom of heaven, but the person who does the will of my Father in heaven."

Commentary: D. Bonhoeffer

We have listened to the Sermon on the Mount and perhaps have understood it. But who has heard it aright? Jesus gives the answer at the end. He does not allow his hearers to go away and make of his sayings what they will, picking and choosing from them whatever they find helpful, and testing them to see if they work. He does not give them free rein to misuse his word with their mercenary hands, but gives it to them on condition that it retains exclusive power over them. Humanly speaking, we could understand and interpret the Sermon on the Mount in a thousand different ways. Jesus knows only one possibility: simple surrender and obedience, not interpreting it or applying it, but doing and obeying it. That is the only way to hear his word. But again he does not mean that it is to be discussed as an ideal; he really means us to get on with it.

This word, whose claim we recognize, this word which issues from his saying *I have known you*, this word which sets us at once to work and obedience, is the rock on which to build our house. The only proper response to this word which Jesus brings with him from eternity is simply to do it. Jesus has spoken: his is the word, ours the obedience. Only in the doing of it does the word of Jesus retain its honor, might and power among us. Now the storm can rage over the house, but it cannot shatter that union with him, which his word has created.

There is only one other possibility, that of failing to do it. It is impossible to want to do it and yet not do it. To deal with the word of Jesus otherwise than by doing it is to give him the lie. It is to deny the Sermon on the Mount and to say "No" to his word. If we start asking questions, posing problems, and offering interpretations, we are not doing his word. Once again the shades of the rich young man and the lawyer of Luke's gospel are raising their heads. However vehemently we assert our faith, and our fundamental recognition of his word, Jesus still calls it "not-doing." But the word which we fail to do is no rock to build a house on. There can then be no union with Jesus. He has never known us. That is why as soon as the hurricane begins we lose the word, and find that we have never really believed it. The word we had was not Christ's, but a word we had wrested from him and made our own by reflecting on it instead of doing it. So our house crashes in ruins, because it is not founded on the word of Jesus Christ.

The multitudes were astonished. . . . What had happened? The Son of God had spoken. He had taken the judgment of the world into his own hands. And his disciples were standing at his side.

(*The Cost of Discipleship*, 218-219)

Dietrich Bonhoeffer (1906-1945), born in Breslau, Germany (then Silesia, Prussia), entered into ministry and studied at the University of Berlin. His thesis for his degree, *Communio Sanctorum*, became very famous then and now because it laid the foundation for all his writings. He studied also at Barcelona, Spain, and the Union Theological Seminary in New York. In 1931 he began teaching at the University of Berlin. In 1933 he was pastor of the German Lutheran congregation in London, but returned to Germany to join the resistance movement. Later he was arrested for his activities in the movement and imprisoned. He was hanged at thirty-nine years of age. While in prison he wrote some beautiful and lasting works. Bonhoeffer's thought has shaped the spirituality of the twentieth century.

Tenth Sunday
in Ordinary Time

Gospel: Matthew 9:9-13

As Jesus was walking on he saw a man named Matthew sitting by the customs house, and he said to him, "Follow me." And he got up and followed him.

Commentary: Y. Congar

Mercy is eminently a quality of God. Saint Irenaeus writes, "To exercise mercy is God's own function," and Saint Catherine of Siena heard God say, "I can be recognized by mercy." But what form does mercy take in God and how does it exist in God? Clearly it is not a passion; God does not undergo an emotional shock and feel sad at the sight of our distress. Mercy exists only in God's will, as a disposition of that will, as an activity of giving, at least if we are thinking of God in his divinity alone. But we know that in Jesus Christ God has attached a manhood to himself, and that he has even revealed the inner secrets of his mystery in that manhood: *Philip, he who has seen me, has seen the Father.*

It is precisely God's humanity and benignity that Jesus Christ revealed. In him God took a human heart and human sensitivity; he was touched, had compassion, and suffered; *he became a merciful and faithful high-priest* . . . It is quite easy and very moving to follow, in the gospels, the abundant signs of the emotion and feeling of mercy which God experienced in the heart and sensitivity of our Lord. Christ understood his mission to be a mission of mercy. He set himself to heal distress of every kind. He described himself with incomparable gentleness as the Good Shepherd: *Come to me, all you who labor and are heavy laden and I will give you rest, for I am meek and humble of heart.* And he said, *I have compassion on the multitude,* not only because it was a flock without a shepherd, but also because it had nothing to eat and seemed unlikely to get anything. He told the parables of mercy. He wept when Lazarus died, and at the thought of the coming destruction of Jerusalem. He was moved by the grief of the widow of Naim, by the centurion's faith, and by that of the Canaanite woman. He forgave the adulterous woman. At the supreme moment of his life he opened eternal life to the thief crucified by his side. He himself experienced the full horror of the death that awaited him: *My soul is sorrowful even unto death.*

In this way, throughout the gospel, God's love, the Father's agape is revealed to us, in the working out of his plan of salvation in the human heart of the incarnate Word. Our own hearts can be moved only by limited amount of distress, and more often by distress we personally dread than by that which is intrinsically more serious. Our compassion is limited by our knowledge, by the very restrictions of our power to love and be generous. But Christ received from God grace, knowledge, and love co-extensive with his mission as universal Savior and his dignity as God made man, with no other boundary, there, than the created world itself.

(The Revelation of God, 54-56)

Yves Congar (1904-   ), a French Dominican, is one of the most respected modern theologians of the Church. He has played a leading role in theological studies, especially in the fields of ecumenism and ecclesiology. He was a peritus at the Second Vatican Council. Father Congar always sought a reformist rather than a revolutionary approach to change in the Church, seeking a change that is progressive and desiring to find the answers to present-day situations in the tradition of the Fathers of the Church. He was ordained a cardinal in 1994 by Pope John Paul II.

Eleventh Sunday in Ordinary Time

Gospel: Matthew 9:36–10:8   When Jesus saw the crowds he felt sorry for them because they were harassed and dejected, like sheep without a shepherd. Then he said to his disciples: "The harvest is rich but the laborers are few."

Commentary: L. Cerfaux

Jesus once composed a set of instructions for his missionaries both present and future. This shall be the subject of our meditation, as it is preserved for us in the gospels, and especially in Matthew's gospel.

Yet this advice was given for only a small mission in Galilee, a trip of a few weeks in the villages of one province. *Do not go among the Gentiles, and do not enter the cities of the Samaritans. Go rather to the lost sheep of the house of Israel, and as you go, preach this message: The kingdom of heaven is at hand!*

Does it matter in the history of the world what a few peasants might say to each other in such a backward corner of the world? Yes, for this was the foundation of the Church, the model of all its missions: the starting point, the nucleus and seed of all that would later develop.

God has a habit of doing great things with nothing. God loves to create. The saints understood this and they accomplished great works with nothing at all, like God, because in their work they followed God's methods. The anchorites of the desert spent their lives battling against the evil spirits. Saint Benedict, driven from Subiaco, founded only the monastery of Monte Cassino. Saint Francis of Assisi formed but a few dozen disciples as guardians of his thought. The Curé of Ars heard confessions in a village church. But it is these humble works which shine. When the apostolate is thus understood, it weighs heavily in the balance of God and the spiritual destiny of the world.

Do you think the noisy apostolate will count for much in the history of the Church? No apostolate, no work, will ever re-echo like the obscure mission of Galilee. And yet what was it in square miles? Galilee is no larger than an American county.

It is neither the surface nor the length nor the width that counts. It is the depth. The apostolate is measured by the plumb line, not the tape measure. *Jesus chose the twelve that they might be always with him, and that he might send them out to preach.*

An apostle is truly an apostle only when he remains united to our Lord. Contemplation and action should not be separated. Mary and Martha are sisters. The two sisters complement each other and make only one. That is how the saints understood it.

For with the saints, too, the apostolate and the interior life are one and the same thing. The holy Curé of Ars could hardly find time to say his prayers, but what a prayer was his life! Saint Francis hesitated his whole life long between the solitude of a hermitage and the work of preaching. Saint Benedict Labré was an apostle by his prayers.

The apostolate is just the glow of sanctity. Apostles should be doubly holy, once for themselves, and once for others.

(Apostle and Apostolate, 1-3)

Lucien Cerfaux (1883-1968) was born in Belgium and studied for the priesthood in Rome. He served as professor of sacred scripture in the seminary of Tournai from 1911 to 1930, in which year he took over the chair of New Testament studies at the Catholic University of Louvain until his retirement in 1964. He served as a peritus at the Second Vatican Council and was a member of the Biblical Commission.

Twelfth Sunday in Ordinary Time

Gospel: Matthew 10:26-33

Jesus said to his disciples: "Do not be afraid of men. For everything that is now covered will be uncovered, and everything now hidden will be made clear."

Commentary: Julian of Norwich

I saw that God rejoices that he is our Father, and God rejoices that he is our Mother, and God rejoices that he is our true spouse, and that our soul is his beloved wife. And Christ rejoices that he is our brother, and Jesus rejoices that he is our savior. These are five great joys, as I understand, in which he wants us to rejoice, praising him, thanking him, loving him, endlessly blessing him, all who will be saved.

During our lifetime here we have in us a marvelous mixture of both well-being and woe. We have in us our risen Lord Jesus Christ, and we have in us the wretchedness and the harm of Adam's falling. Dying, we are constantly protected by Christ, and by the touching of his grace we are raised to true trust in salvation. And we are so afflicted in our feelings by Adam's falling in various ways, by sin and by different pains, and in this we are made dark and so blind that we can scarcely accept any comfort. But in our intention we wait for God, and trust faithfully to have mercy and grace; and this is his own working in us, and in his goodness he opens the eye of our understanding, by which we have sight, sometimes more and sometimes less, according to the ability God gives us to receive. And now we are raised to the one, and now we are permitted to fall to the other. And so that mixture is so marvelous in us that we scarcely know, about ourselves or about our fellow Christians, what condition we are in, these conflicting feelings are so extraordinary, except for each holy act of assent to God which we make when we feel him, truly willing with all our heart to be with him, and with all our soul and with all our might. And then we hate and despise our evil inclinations, and everything which could be an occasion of spiritual and bodily sin. And even so, when this sweetness is hidden, we fall again into blindness, and so in various ways into woe and tribulation. But then this is our comfort, that we know in our faith that by the power of Christ who is our protector we never assent to that, but we complain about it, and endure in pain and in woe, praying until the time that he shows himself again to us. And so we remain in this mixture all the days of our life; but he wants us to trust that he is constantly with us, and that in three ways.

He is with us in heaven, true man in his own person, drawing us up; and that was revealed in the spiritual thirst. And he is with us on earth, leading us; and that was revealed in the third revelation, where I saw God in a moment of time. And he is with us in our soul, endlessly dwelling, ruling and guarding.

(Showings, 279-280)

Julian, an anchoress who lived in solitude in Norwich, England, in the late fourteenth century, received the sixteen "showings" or revelations of God's love in a series of experienced visions. Julian's writings reveal a person who experienced God directly and not self-consciously as "our mother." Her revelations of the feminine side of God represent a significant contribution to the tradition. Her graphic visions of the humanity of Christ are marked by vivid imagery and detail. But the special appeal of Julian lies in her theology of the all-embracing fullness of divine love.

Thirteenth Sunday in Ordinary Time

Gospel: Matthew 10:37-42   Jesus said to his disciples: "Anyone who prefers father or mother to me is not worthy of me."

Commentary: R. Guardini

The message of Jesus is one of good will. He proclaims the Father's love and the advent of his kingdom. He calls people to the peace and harmony of life lived in the divine will. Yet their first reaction is not union, but division. The more profoundly Christian a man becomes, the deeper the cleft between him and those who refuse to follow Christ—its exact measure proportionate to that refusal. The split runs right through the most intimate relationship, for genuine conversion is not a thing of natural disposition or historical development, but the most personal decision an individual can make. The one makes it, the other does not; hence the possibility of a schism between father and son, friend and friend, one member of a household and another. When it comes to a choice between domestic peace and Jesus, one must value Jesus higher, even higher than the most dearly beloved: father and mother, son and daughter, friend or love. This means cutting into the very core of life, and temptation presses us to preserve human ties and abandon Christ. But Jesus warns us: If you hold "life" fast, sacrificing me for it, you lose your own true life. If you let it go for my sake, you will find yourself in the heart of immeasurable reality.

Naturally this is difficult; it is the cross. And here we touch the heaviest mystery of Christianity, its inseparableness from Calvary. Ever since Christ walked the way of the cross, it stands firmly planted on every Christian's road, for every follower of Christ has his own personal cross. Nature revolts against it, wishing to "preserve" herself. She tries to go around it, but Jesus has said unequivocally, and his words are fundamental to Christianity: He who hangs on, body and soul, to "life" will lose it; he who surrenders his will to his cross will find it—once and for ever in the immortal self that shares in the life of Christ.

On the last journey to Jerusalem, shortly before the Transfiguration, Christ's words about the cross are repeated. Then, sharply focused, comes the new thought: *For what does it profit a man, if he gain the whole world, but suffer the loss of his own soul? Or what will a man give in exchange for his soul?*

This time the point plunges deeper. The dividing line runs not between one person and another, but between the believer or one desirous of belief, and everything else. Between me and the world. Between me and myself. The lesson of the cross is the great lesson of self-surrender and self-conquest.

(The Lord, 292-293)

Romano Guardini (1885-1968), born at Verona in Italy, grew up in Mainz and was ordained in 1910. Ten years later he was admitted to the faculty of divinity at Bonn. In 1923 he became professor of dogmatic theology at Breslau and in 1945 professor of philosophy at Tübingen. His books were widely read by the laity and had great influence especially on the younger generation. They include: *The Lord, The Faith and Modern Man, The Living God,* and *Sacred Signs.*

Fourteenth Sunday in Ordinary Time

Gospel: Matthew 11:25-30   Jesus exclaimed: "I bless you, Father, Lord of heaven and of earth, for hiding these things from the learned and clever and revealing them to mere children."

Commentary: Abhishiktananda   *Yes, Father, for that is what it pleased you to do* . . . The kingdom of heaven is actually hidden from the wise and prudent of this world, even from the many who proclaim themselves spiritual. They are too rich to accept the constant gift of God, they are too intelligent to say with the babes, *Yes, Father*, and above all to say it, not with so-called resignation or acceptance under compulsion, but with the same joy which was prompted in the heart of Christ by his discovering in everything the love of the Father.

For him who has faith everything comes from the Father and everything leads to the Father. Health, sickness, wealth, poverty, success, failure, and so on, are only manifestations of the holy will of God. After all, was the Father showing less love to his beloved Son when he allowed him to be condemned and crucified than when he gave him to Mary to be fed and caressed by her?

It is an act of prayer and contemplation to look at the sun, at the stars, at the sky, when faith reveals in them the presence and love of the Creator, since through them God prepared the earth to be the cradle of humankind and the place of the incarnation. Is it not through the sun particularly, through its light and heat, that life was made possible here below for the children of the Father, and especially for his first-born, the Lord Jesus, who blessed the sun forever with his divine glance? There is indeed nothing in the world whose impact on our senses should not blossom into prayer, when looked at with the eyes of faith, with the eyes of Christ, the one who knows everything *in the Father*. It could even be said that through our eyes and all our senses it is God himself who is looking at his own creation and taking delight in it, who sees that it is all good.

To pray without ceasing is not so much consciously to think of God as to allow Jesus to live freely in us his life as the Son of God. It is to be attentive to the Father who comes to us by any path he may choose. It is to hear in all creatures and every event the call which comes to us from the eternity of God, the "Thou" which the Father addresses mysteriously to each one of us within the "Thou"—*Thou art my beloved Son*—by which he calls his Son and pours out his love upon him. It is to answer with Christ in the Holy Spirit, *Abba, Father*, out of the love of our hearts in every act of our conscious life.

(Prayer, 18-19)

Abhishiktananda (1910-1973), born Henri le Saux in Brittany, entered the monastery of Saint Anne de Kergonan in 1929. Quite early in his monastic life he felt drawn to India and in 1945 he was allowed to approach Indian bishops. In 1947 he received a favorable reply from the bishop of Tirnchirappali, and together with a secular priest, Jules Monchanin who was already in the diocese, started an ashram called Shantivanam, integrating elements of Indian sannyasa with Christian monasticism. Dom Henri, who adopted the Indian name Abhishiktananda (Bliss of the Anointed One), was at this time profoundly influenced by a contemporary holy man, Sri Ramana Maharshi, and through him was initiated into the Hindu tradition of "advaita" or non-duality. The rest of his life was a struggle to integrate this experience into his Christianity. In the end he achieved it, not on the conceptual level but in the inner peace of his own prayer. His chief works are *Prayer, Saccidananda, Hindu-Christian Meeting Point*, and *The Further Shore*.

Fifteenth Sunday in Ordinary Time

Gospel: Matthew 13:1-23

Jesus left the house and sat by the lakeside, but such crowds gathered round him that he got into a boat and sat there. He told them many things in parables. "Imagine a sower going out to sow."

Commentary: L. Fonck

Our Lord by this beautiful simile willed to teach a twofold lesson to his disciples and to those who were with them. In the first place, he shows them by his choice of the image that his kingdom will not be suddenly proclaimed in power and splendor. The word of the Kingdom resembles rather the small and insignificant grain of wheat which is committed to the earth to develop therein slowly and gradually, and to yield a rich harvest in the good ground.

Our Lord in this first parable gives chief importance to another lesson. He shows in the second place whence comes the opposition to the word of the Kingdom and the partial unproductiveness of the good seed. He had before all things himself, his work, and its results before his eyes. It happened with his message of the kingdom of God upon earth in Israel as with the seed in the ground. It is in the similarity of their fate and the partial productiveness and non-productiveness of both that the point of comparison lies in this parable.

By means of the explanation of the reason for the unbelief in Israel the scandal which might prove a stumbling block to the disciples is removed. And, on the other hand, the mysterious gradual development of God's kingdom is vividly illustrated in an extremely suggestive and instructive manner. At the same time the words of the divine Master contain for each individual an earnest exhortation to self-examination and the avoidance of these obstacles.

The fundamental idea here set forth shows us, also, how beautifully the lesson which our Lord intended rules the similitude and its interpretation in all their parts. As our Lord himself explained every point, we have but to consider his words carefully without seeking further elucidation.

The first obstacle whereby a portion of the seed was rendered unproductive was the hard, much trodden way. By this our Lord teaches us to recognize the first class of listeners to his Word, who hear it indeed, but do not understand. At the same time we are to regard this want of understanding as their own fault. They hear the word and take no trouble to accept it and to attend to it. It is true the disciples did not understand the parable, but they went with goodwill to their divine Master and begged an explanation. On the other hand, indifference and coldness of heart toward the teaching of their Redeemer was in the case of many of the unbelieving people the principal cause of their unbelief. Their hearts were like the hard path through the field on the surface of which the seed remained.

(The Parables of the Gospel, 87-88)

Leopold Fonck (1865-1930), born in Wissen, Germany, studied at Kempen, Germany, and the Gregorian University in Rome. He was ordained in 1889 and entered the Society of Jesus in 1892. After embarking on a career in biblical studies, he taught New Testament exegesis at the University of Innsbruck from 1901 to 1908, when he was invited to the Gregorian. In 1909 he founded the Pontifical Biblical Institute and was its first rector and also prepared the founding of a filial institute in Jerusalem. His last years were spent in Prague and Vienna where he devoted himself to the ministry.

Sixteenth Sunday in Ordinary Time

Gospel: Matthew 13:24-43   Jesus put a parable before the crowds, "The kingdom of heaven may be compared to a man who sowed good seed in his field."

Commentary: R. Knox

*T*he parable of the wheat and the cockle is really one of a pair; people often do not realize that, because the sister parable does not follow straight on it, but at an interval of several verses, though they are both in the same chapter. The sister parable, as I call it, is the one in which our Lord compares the kingdom of heaven to a net which is let down into the sea and draws up a great quantity of fish, both bad and good. Either parable is an answer to the question, "Do all Christians go to heaven?" And the answer is "No." And if you ask why, either parable supplies the same explanation; God does not want it to be known in this life which souls are his and which will meet with final rejection; it is better for our faith that we should belong to a Church which has imperfect as well as perfect members; better for our watchfulness over ourselves that we should realize the possibility of being a baptized Christian, and yet not bound for heaven.

Let me draw that out a little. The field in which the wheat and cockle are sown is the world; our Lord has told us that; but the crop of grain, bad and good alike, is, I think, the Church. It is in the Church, not simply in the world, that bad and good grow together side by side. And the servants of the householder, that is the angels, are represented as saying: *Shall we root up the cockle*; shall we exterminate the wicked, as they were exterminated at the time of the deluge, and leave only the righteous to live? And they are told: *No, wait till the harvest*, that is till the judgment, and then the distinction will be made clear; then shall the just shine forth in the kingdom of their Father. So in the other parable, good and worthless fish alike must be carried in the net; it is only when the boat reaches the shore that they will be separated, and the worthless fish thrown away; till then you will have people who wear the sign of Christ on their foreheads and take his name on their lips, but who will not be able to resign their souls into his hands with full contrition, at the last terrible moment of their lives.

If every pope had become impeccable at the moment when he became infallible, and Alexander VI had turned into a Savanarola at the instant when the triple tiara was put on his head; if all the triumphs of the Church had been achieved bloodlessly and all had been utilized immediately for the evident good of mankind; if there had never been such a thing as a worldly bishop, or an idle monk or faithless friar, would it not all be too obvious, too plain sailing? Our Lord, it is quite evident, did not contemplate anything of that kind. It is necessary to the world, he said, necessary that scandals should come; it is part of our probation, he would have us understand, that we should be puzzled by these anomalies of religious history and distressed by them, and yet have enough strength of resolution to see behind them and beyond them, and recognize the Church as his own bride, the inheritor of his promises and the completion of his life.

(*University and Anglican Sermons*, 65-68)

Ronald Knox (1881-1951), son of E. A. Knox, one-time bishop of Manchester, England, was educated at Eton and Oxford. Already noted for the brilliance of his mind, he was appointed chaplain of Trinity College, Oxford, and became a leading figure among Anglo-Catholics. In 1917 he was received into the Roman Catholic Church and ordained two years later. He taught for a time at Saint Edmund's Ware and was chaplain to the Catholic undergraduates at Oxford from 1936 to 1939. At the request of the hierarchy he then devoted himself to making a new English translation of the entire bible. The New Testament was first published in 1945 and the Old in 1949. As a writer on a wide range of subjects, Knox's thought is often strikingly original and his style characterized by wit.

Seventeenth Sunday in Ordinary Time

Gospel: Matthew 13:44-52   Jesus said: "The kingdom of heaven is like a treasure hidden in a field which someone has found."

Commentary: E. Armstrong

*I*n a peasant community there were difficulties in storing valuables. The poor man's safe was the earth. During turbulent times wealthy people, too, buried their treasures, and sometimes misadventures or the ravages of war prevented them from returning to retrieve what they had buried. A treasure trove was uncovered every now and then, and tales about fortunate finders were retailed by wishful thinkers throughout the countryside. In folktales the virtuous are sometimes rewarded by coming on hidden treasure, as in the rabbinic story of the good fortune which befell Abba Judan after he had philanthropically given all he possessed, except a cow and a field, to the needy. The cow fell into a hole in the field, breaking its leg, but in trying to rescue it Abba Judan found an immense treasure. In our sophisticated society only children can believe that a crock of gold is to be found at the foot of the rainbow, but a fortunate farmer may still unearth a treasure, while he is plowing, as at Mildenhall, in Suffolk, when magnificently ornate Roman silver dishes were uncovered. In 1952 two heavily oxidized copper rolls were discovered at Qumran near the Dead Sea. The inscriptions recorded where treasures had been secreted, but diligent search revealed nothing.

Attention has been called to material differences between this parable and the version in Thomas and a rabbinic story. The latter, commenting on Song of Songs 4:12, recounts the history of a man who inherited a place full of rubbish. "The inheritor was lazy and sold it for a ridiculously small sum. The purchaser dug there industriously and found in it a treasure. He built therewith a great palace and passed through the bazaar with a train of slaves which he had bought with the treasure. When the seller saw it he could have choked himself (out of chagrin)." Here the common folk-theme of the lazy or ignorant simpleton appears. In the Gospel of Thomas a son sells the land inherited from his father and the purchaser plows it, finds the treasure, and becomes a moneylender. The contrast between these and the gospel parable is immense.

The parable of the peerless pearl is twin to the hidden treasure, and the two may have been told together; for parallelism is a characteristic of Hebrew style, both in short clauses and in more elaborate compositions: *If a kingdom be divided against itself, that kingdom cannot stand. And if a house be divided against itself, that house cannot stand.*

The discoverer of the treasure trove was a comparatively poor man who chanced on the money; the pearl merchant was relatively wealthy; he came on the pearl in the course of business and sold his whole stock to acquire it. One man enters into the joy of the kingdom unexpectedly, another gains it through the maturing of a lifetime's endeavor. Unlike the rich young ruler, when the supreme opportunity presented itself the pearl merchant was ready to invest everything. We are given to understand that his life had been devoted to acquiring ever more perfect pearls. Each, in turn, was a joyful attainment. So should the Christian's life be attuned to anticipating the insights and inspirations God gives as life goes on, confident that He has still finer things to reveal to us. We may not all have unexpected, glorious, mystical experiences, but we should aspire after clearer insights, some of which may have at least a little of the quality of that ecstasy enjoyed by Pascal. Sewn into his doublet, when he lay dead, was found this testimony: *Certitude, perception, joy, peace, . . . joy, joy, joy, tears of joy.*

(*The Gospel Parables,* 154-157)

Edward A. Armstrong (1900-1978), born in Belfast, Northern Ireland, studied at Queen's University, Belfast, Ridley Hall, Cambridge, Hong Kong University (Chinese studies), and the University of Leeds. An Anglican clergyman, he had a great interest in ornithology and wrote many books and articles on this subject. He also wrote religious books.

Eighteenth Sunday in Ordinary Time

Gospel: Matthew 14:13-21

Jesus withdrew by boat to a lonely place where they could be by themselves. But the people heard of this and, leaving the towns, went after him on foot.

Commentary: D. E. Garland

We see Jesus, who did not do many miracles in Nazareth because of lack of faith, performing miracles for the crowds because of their faith. For Matthew, faith is confidence in Jesus' power. The crowds' faith in Jesus is implied by the fact that they do the same things that others, inspired by faith, have done earlier in the narrative. They bring to him all those who were sick like the men who brought the paralytic to Jesus. They believe that they can be healed by touching the fringe of Jesus' garment, like the woman with the hemorrhage who touched Jesus' garment. Their faith in Jesus' power contrasts with the little faith of the disciples, who appear to lack that same confidence.

The fast approaching evening prompts the disciples to implore Jesus to send the crowds off into the villages to secure something to eat for themselves. Jesus' command, *You give them something to eat,* is met with a helpless response that they have only limited resources, five loaves and two fishes. They doubt Jesus' divine power in their midst to supply whatever is needed to feed the crowd as Moses doubted God's power in the wilderness. They will slowly begin to learn of Jesus' capacity to supply in abundance and of their task to feed the people.

The miracle of the loaves and fishes also lends itself to several other impressions. It recalls the exodus theme, where Israel is fed in the wilderness. The abundance may signify the presence of the messianic age and salvation: "And it shall come to pass at the self-same time that the treasury of manna shall again descend from on high, and they will eat of it in those years, because these are they who have come to the consummation of time." The parallels with the narrative of the Lord's supper may suggest that Jesus is the source of spiritual nourishment. The feeding of five thousand with the excess collected in twelve baskets indicates the abundant supply of all Israel. The eucharist, however, will offer bread for all humankind.

The story also bears witness once again to Jesus' compassion for the needy: they do not have to be sent away hungry. Jesus has compassion for their needs as God does: *The afflicted shall eat and be satisfied. And I will set up my servant David, and he shall feed them; he shall feed them and be their shepherd.*

After the miracle of the feeding, Jesus compels his disciples to get into the boat and go before him to the other side while he dismisses the crowd. The narrator offers no clue as to why Jesus does this, but their departure in the boat means that they will experience a divine manifestation apart from the crowds. When Jesus disperses the crowds, he ascends a mountain to pray privately.

(Reading Matthew, 155-156)

David E. Garland (1921-   ), a graduate of The Southern Baptist Theological Seminary, has served as interim pastor in Kentucky and Indiana in addition to his teaching at The Southern Baptist Theological Seminary. He has authored many articles and six books on scripture.

Nineteenth Sunday in Ordinary Time

Gospel: Matthew 14:22-33

Jesus made the disciples get into the boat and go on ahead to the other side while he would send the crowds away. After sending the crowds away he went up into the hills by himself to pray.

Commentary: R. Guardini

When Jesus reassures the frightened disciples that it is indeed he who is walking on the water and not a ghost, Peter says: *Lord, if it is you, bid me come to you over the water.* What do the words reveal? The desire for proof, and we admire the boldness of that desire, for if it is a ghost that stands there, the proof will be fatal; it is also evidence of faith. So Jesus calls: *Come!* Peter, his eyes deep in the eyes of the Lord, steps overboard and sets his foot upon a wave. The water bears his weight. He believes. To believe means to share not what Christ believes, but what he is. Thus Peter participates in Jesus' act. But all divine action is living action, that rises and falls. As long as Peter's gaze holds that of the Master and his faith remains one with the divine will, the water carries him. Then the tension of his trust slackens, consciousness of his human limitations surges in on him and he recalls the power of the elements. He hears the roar of the wind and feels the waves rock beneath his feet. This is the moment of crisis. Instead of leaning more heavily on the support from Jesus' gaze, Peter drops his eyes. Contact with the divine strength is severed and he starts to sink. All that remains of the fleeting, world-conquering faith is the helpless cry: *Lord, save me!*

The passage contains one of the most important revelations of the nature of faith. What the believing soul experiences is not a "truth" or a "value," but a reality—the reality. Which? The reality of God in the living Christ. In the midst of everything that man may think or experience, in the midst of all that is known as the "world," there rises a point that does not belong to the world, a place into which one may step, a room one may enter, a power on which one may lean, a love to which one may give oneself. This is reality, a reality different from the reality of the world, more real than the world. Faith is the act of seizing this reality, of building one's life on it, of becoming part of it.

(*The Lord*, 198-199)

Romano Guardini (1885-1968), born at Verona in Italy, grew up in Mainz and was ordained in 1910. Ten years later he was admitted to the faculty of divinity at Bonn. In 1923 he became professor of dogmatic theology at Breslau and in 1945 professor of philosophy at Tübingen. His books were widely read by the laity and had great influence especially on the younger generation. They include: *The Lord, The Faith and Modern Man, The Living God,* and *Sacred Signs.*

Twentieth Sunday in Ordinary Time

Gospel: Matthew 15:21-28

Jesus withdrew to the region of Tyre and Sidon. Then out came a Canaanite woman from that district and started shouting: "Sir, Son of David, take pity on me. My daughter is tormented by a devil."

Commentary: Thomas of Villanova

The Canaanite woman did not have the law, she did not know the prophets, she was unacquainted with the mysteries, and yet, good God, how many virtues and signs suddenly shine forth from her! What faith, what trust, what patience, what humility, what perseverance! She had not seen Christ's miracles, she had not witnessed the dead rising, the blind seeing, the deaf hearing, the lame leaping; but at the hearing of some light rumor, faith filled her godly heart, and she believed with a firm devotion of soul that her absent, demon possessed daughter could be healed by his word alone. Her trust in obtaining his favor was so strong that she neither became silent when scorned nor gave up when despised. She had cried out with incredible patience, and the Lord ignored her. He continued on and did not answer her. He pushed aside the interceding apostles. He reviled her as she was praying and lying prostrate before him. No one was ever exasperated, no one ever scorned, no one ever provoked by so many rebukes.

What can I say of her humility? When she was called a dog, she also added her own abuse and called herself a puppy. Her perseverance was beyond human ability, for as often as she was provoked and despised, she never ceased from crying out until she obtained her request. O the wonderful greenness of this bough! O this remarkable woman, firmer in faith than one of the faithful, more filled with virtues than someone initiated in the mysteries!

What shall you say, O faithful soul, when you grow cold and numb, you who are imbued with the sacraments of life from the beginning, who are among so many teachings of holy scriptures, among so many oracles of prophets and apostles, among holy rites every day and continuous praises of God, among frequent sermons on the divine law and constant exhortations of preachers? Learn fervency from this idolater, learn faith, learn virtue.

The Lord knew what lay hidden within her. He kept silent that she might become known; he disdained her that she might shine; he delayed that he might exalt her, that he might leave behind for the Church this woman as an example for imitation, that he might provide all future generations with this exemplar of all virtues. He suddenly confirmed her, not with an external word, but with an internal ray; thus rightly the Church presents her now to the penitent, that they might see in her what they should follow, that they might observe in her what they should imitate.

O sinner, do for your own soul what she did for her daughter. For your soul suffers with a similar sickness, it is weighed down by an equal infirmity, it is vexed by an evil demon in the same way. Run, then, for healing, seek a cure, cry out, beg, and keep at it. Do what she did and you will be free, just as her daughter was freed.

(*Sermons, Thursday after the First Sunday of Lent,* Sermon 2)

Thomas of Villanova (1486-1555) abandoned an academic career to become in 1516 an Augustinian friar, and was made a prior before long. In 1533 while prior provincial he sent friars to the New World. After having declined the see of Granada, he was put under obedience to accept the archbishopric of Valencia which had been so neglected that he was excused from attending the Council of Trent. His time and money were devoted to the poor and the sick, and to ransoming captives, so that he was called the Beggar Bishop, father of the poor. His many sermons had an influence on Spanish spiritual literature: particularly notable is one on the love of God, and in another he wrote of the conception of our Lady as most holy, without stain.

Twenty-First Sunday in Ordinary Time

Gospel: Matthew 16:13-20   When Jesus came to the region of Caesarea Philippi he put this question to his disciples: "Who do people say the Son of Man is?"

Commentary: Paul VI

To speak of Jesus as he appears in the course of the gospel has become something very attractive, inevitable, and compelling, but at the same time, difficult and ambiguous. So much so indeed, that the question: "Who is Jesus?" lent itself to the most varied answers, and even in the minds of the disciples it was not at all clear who he might be. Then it was, you remember, that Jesus, going along with the same little group of disciples toward Caesarea Philippi, in the north of Palestine near Mount Hermon, puts to them a searching question: *Who do men say that the Son of Man is?* After a variety of confused answers, taken from public opinion, Jesus pressed home the point of the discourse by putting the straight question to his future apostles: *But who do you say that I am?* Then it was that Peter, enlightened by God the Father, replies, surely also in the name of the rest, and gives the famous, invincible definition of Jesus: *You are the Christ, the Son of the living God!*

Let us all hold fast in thought, in heart, in life, to this most certain and ineffable truth about our Lord Jesus Christ, one in the divine Person of the only-begotten Son of God; eternal in the nature of the Word, incarnate in human nature in Mary by the operation of the Holy Spirit. Let us remember the reality of this mystery, overshadowing all history and all the destiny of the human race, the mystery of the unique person of the Word of God, living in the divine nature and in the human nature of Jesus. It is the supreme dogma which we profess at Mass every Sunday and every feast day when we sing the creed. It is the foundation of our Christian faith and of our salvation.

Let us all remember the confession of Peter which we have professed with explicit adherence and inexhaustible joy here upon his tomb, in the certainty that, founded upon the apostolic rock and on the cornerstone which is Christ himself, the building which he, using us as living stones, is now constructing, cannot fall, either with the passing of time or with death which seems to destroy all things. This building is his Church, holy and immortal, to which we have the good fortune to belong and from which we receive Christ himself, the bread of eternal life.

Here faith appears in its supreme importance and necessity, in its origin as an active gift of God, and as a humble and sincere beginning reminding us of his Word. With an act of faith, that is, of acceptance of divine Truth which transcends our cognitive or experimental powers, let us salute Jesus Christ, once again with the words of Simon Peter: *Lord, to whom shall we go? You have the words of eternal life. And we have believed and have come to know that you are the Christ, the Son of God.*

(*Discourses*, 27 April 1975)

Paul VI (1897-1978), born Giovanni Battista Montini, was ordained a priest in 1920 and in 1925 entered the Vatican Secretariat of State. In this service of the Church he filled several important posts until he was named archbishop of Milan by Pius XII on 1 November 1954. Montini was made a cardinal in December 1958, and elected pope on 21 June 1963. During his long pontificate he showed himself to be an intrepid pastor and a determined promoter of the decrees of the Second Vatican Council. In spite of opposition he firmly held the bark of Peter on its course into a new age.

Twenty-Second Sunday in Ordinary Time

Gospel: Matthew 16:21-27

Jesus began to make it clear to his disciples that he was destined to go to Jerusalem and suffer grievously at the hands of the elders and chief priests and scribes, to be put to death and to be raised up on the third day.

Commentary: C. Lubich

*L*et him take up his cross. . . . These are strange and unique words, which like all words said by Jesus, have something in them of a light which this world does not know. They are so luminous that they dazzle and, therefore, blind the blank, sleep-ridden eyes of people, including those of apathetic Christians.

Perhaps there is nothing more enigmatic, more difficult to grasp, than the cross. It is not understood because we are Christians only in name—baptized, yes, maybe even practicing Christians, yet immensely far from being what Jesus would like us to be.

We hear about the cross in Lent. We sing hymns about it on Good Friday and sometimes we hang it up in our rooms. It is the sign with which we place a seal on many of our activities. Yet it is not understood.

And perhaps the mistake lies in the fact that love is not understood in this world. Love is the finest of words, but it is also the most misused and debased. It is the essence of God, the life itself of the children of God, the breath of the Christian. Yet this word has been taken over by the world. It is on the lips of those who have no right to it.

But the love that is not understood is Love itself—the fact that God who made us, who came on earth as a man among men and women, lived with us and allowed himself to be nailed to a cross in order to save us. This love is too high and beautiful, too divine and too far above our human loves, too blood-stained and painful to be understood by us.

The cross is the necessary instrument whereby the divine penetrates into what is human, and humanity participates more fully in God's life, entering into the kingdom of heaven already on this earth.

But we really have to take up our cross. We must get up in the morning expecting it, and knowing that only by means of it can we receive those gifts which this world does not have—peace and joy, knowledge of the things of heaven which are unknown to most people.

The cross is such a common thing. It never fails to come day by day. Taking this cross as it comes would be enough to make us saints. The cross is the emblem of the Christian. The world does not want it because it believes that it will avoid suffering by fleeing from the cross. People do not know that the cross opens wide the soul of the person who has understood it to the kingdom of light and love, to the love which this world is always seeking, but does not possess.

(Meditations, 10-13)

Chiara Lubich (1920-   ), born in Trent, Italy, is the foundress and president of the Focolare whose spirituality of unity has benefited millions of people of all races and cultures. She is a member of the Pontifical Council of the Laity, and a leading figure in world ecumenism. In 1977 she was awarded the Templeton Prize for the progress of religions and currently she is an honorary president of the World Council of Religions for Peace.

Twenty-Third Sunday in Ordinary Time

Gospel: Matthew 18:15-20

Jesus said to his disciples: "If your brother does something wrong, go and have it out with him alone, between your two selves. If he listens to you, you have won back your brother."

Commentary: B. Rigaux

The first part of the communitarian instruction of chapter 18 gives instructions to the disciples regarding their relationship to the "little children." The exposition of his literary composition concludes with the following instructions: 1) A little child must be welcomed because of my name; and in welcoming him, you are welcoming me. 2) You must become like one of these little ones; whoever is humble like this little child, he is the greatest in the kingdom of heaven. It is a question therefore of meriting entrance into the eschatological kingdom and, by meriting, being welcomed into it by Jesus. 3) You must not be an obstacle to one of these little ones *who have faith in me.* 4) You must not despise one of these little ones: *For I tell you that their angels in heaven are continually in the presence of my Father in heaven.*

The last two uses of "little ones" leads the discourse back to the plane of the prerequisites of the community. From the "little one" who is a child, we go on to *the little ones who have faith in me.* Who are those who give scandal? Matthew has named the disciples, but we know that, with him, disciple often designates the twelve, the leaders. As in Matthew 18:15-22, four pericopes are addressed to the community: brotherly correction, to bind and to loosen, prayer in common, and forgiveness of injuries. We can believe that *these little ones who have faith in me* form a part of that community: Christians whose faith is not total; Christians of humble status, simple, poor, sinners; the mass of the faithful in opposition to these disciples-leaders, who must not give scandal. Matthew's Church appears, as it is described elsewhere, as a divided Church about to collapse. We understand then why after the "little ones" the gospel reports the parable of the lost sheep, the mention of brotherly correction, the power to forgive sins, to forgive seventy-seven times, and the parable of the unforgiving debtor.

There is the same perspective in the pericope (Matthew 18:18) where with solemnity and authority Jesus proclaims: *Whatever you bind on earth shall be considered bound in heaven; what you loose on earth shall be considered loosed in heaven.*

In itself, this power of excommunication and of pardon applies here to the entire Church. Nevertheless in Matthew 16:19, these words are quoted to confer a special power on Peter. The expression "on earth" recalls the power given to men, which was evoked after Jesus had forgiven the sins of the paralytic. If we bear in mind the era when Matthew was written and the existence in this community of a penitential discipline, the Church, the last court of appeal, does indeed seem to be the authoritative recipient of the power of the keys. Authority in the Church is not anonymous or diffused. A community does not exist without a leader, without a president. The organization of the Palestinian and Pauline communities are proof of this.

The prayer "on earth" heard by the Father because *where two or three meet in my name, I shall be there with them,* ushers us into a group assembled for the celebration of the liturgy.

The Church is a community where men and women sin, where I must forgive my brother who "wrongs me" up to seventy-seven times. The parable of the unforgiving debtor also applies not to the future kingdom of heaven but to present conditions: a brother or sister must forgive often and from the heart.

(*The Testimony of Saint Matthew,* 149-151)

Béda Rigaux is a scholar, exegete, and historian. He received his doctorate from the University of Louvain in 1932 and taught for years at this university. Outstanding among his published works are *The Letters to the Thessalonians,* an indispensable commentary for biblical scholars of every persuasion, and his very fine work, *The Letters of Saint Paul.*

Twenty-Fourth Sunday in Ordinary Time

Gospel: Matthew 18:21-35

Peter went up to Jesus and said, "Lord, how often must I forgive my brother if he wrongs me? As often as seven times?" Jesus answered, "Not seven, I tell you, but seventy-seven times seven."

Commentary: M. L. King

During his ministry in the sunny villages of Galilee, Jesus talked passionately about forgiveness. This strange doctrine awakened the questioning mind of Peter. *How oft,* he asked, *shall my brother sin against me, and I forgive him? till seven times?* Peter wanted to be legal and statistical. But Jesus responded by affirming that there is no limit to forgiveness. *I say not unto thee, Until seven times: but, Until seventy times seven.* In other words, forgiveness is not a matter of quantity, but of quality. A man cannot forgive up to four hundred and ninety times without forgiveness becoming a part of the habit structure of his being. Forgiveness is not an occasional act; it is a permanent attitude.

Jesus also admonished his followers to love their enemies and to pray for them that despitefully used them. This teaching fell upon the ears of many of his hearers like a strange music from a foreign land. Their ears were not attuned to the tonal qualities of such amazing love. They had been taught to love their friends and hate their enemies. Their lives had been conditioned to seek redress in the time-honored tradition of retaliation. Yet Jesus taught them that only through a creative love for their enemies could they be children of their Father in heaven and also that love and forgiveness were absolute necessities for spiritual maturity.

Let us be practical and ask the question, How do we love our enemies? First, we must develop and maintain the capacity to forgive. He who is devoid of the power to forgive is devoid of the power to love. It is impossible even to begin the act of loving one's enemies without the prior acceptance of the necessity, over and over again, of forgiving those who inflict evil and injury upon us. It is also necessary to realize that the forgiving act must always be initiated by the person who has been wronged, the victim of some great hurt, the recipient of some tortuous injustice, the absorber of some terrible act of oppression. The wrongdoer may request forgiveness. He may come to himself, and, like the prodigal son, move up some dusty road, his heart palpitating with the desire for forgiveness. But only the injured neighbor, the loving father back home, can really pour out the warm waters of forgiveness.

Forgiveness does not mean ignoring what has been done or putting a false label on an evil act. It means, rather, that the evil act no longer remains as a barrier to the relationship. Forgiveness is a catalyst creating the atmosphere necessary for a fresh start and a new beginning. It is the lifting of a burden or the canceling of a debt. The words "I will forgive you, but I'll never forget what you've done" never explain the real nature of forgiveness. Certainly one can never forget, if that means erasing it totally from his mind. But when we forgive, we forget in the sense that the evil deed is no longer a mental block impeding a new relationship. Likewise, we can never say, "I will forgive you, but I won't have anything further to do with you." Forgiveness means reconciliation, a coming together again. Without this, no man can love his enemies. The degree to which we are able to forgive determines the degree to which we are able to love our enemies.

(Strength to Love, 26-27.35)

Martin Luther King (1929-1968) was born in Atlanta, Georgia, USA, and in 1954 accepted a call to Dexter Avenue Baptist Church. He became involved in racial equality and organized many events to make people become more aware of this pressing problem. Notable among events were the March on Washington and the Selma Demonstration. He was assassinated on the balcony of a hotel in Memphis, Tennessee, on 4 April 1968, but his legacy continues to live on.

Twenty-Fifth Sunday in Ordinary Time

Gospel: Matthew 20:1-16

Jesus said to his disciples: "The kingdom of heaven is like a landowner going out at daybreak to hire workers for his vineyard."

Commentary: K. Rahner

*I*t seems to me that this gospel of the laborers in the vineyard, even though we know it so well, appears stranger and more incomprehensible each time it is read. That every man receives the same reward surely does not hold true of eternity. Nor can we conclude from this story that God does not render to every man according to his works, for it is written in scripture that he does. What then, we may well ask, is this story really telling us?

The householder expressly asks the grumblers whether he has not the right to be generous. What he gives to the latecomers, therefore, is not an expression of wages which they have earned or of the justice which applies to masters and servants; rather it is an expression of his own generosity, that free generosity—and here we are coming to the point of the whole story—that incalculable mercy, that grace which cannot be reckoned up in terms of wages and justice, that generosity and mercy which ultimately prevails between God and man.

Where it is that this mercy of God enters our life, where it is that he shows himself to us as one who freely disposes of us and does not negotiate, is an entirely different question. We cannot find the answer to it in this parable. We cannot make an unjustified application of the details of this parable to the divine reality. We can only say that in the last analysis everything we can earn and must earn in the way of wages depends on the free disposition of God, who gives to us as he wills and ordains our beginning and our ending according to his pleasure. From this there follows something which can never, I think, lose its importance for us.

The thing which God freely disposes of, the thing we cannot

negotiate or calculate about with him, is ultimately our own selves. Our own selves, just as we are: with our life, with our temperament, with our destiny, with our surroundings, with our time, with our heredity, with our family, with everything that we happen to be and cannot change. And whenever we grumble and complain about others with whom God has dealt differently, we are really refusing to accept our own selves from the hands of God. This parable teaches us to say: we are those who receive the denarius, we ourselves are the denarius. For we receive ourselves, with our destiny, with our freedom certainly and whatever we choose to do with that freedom, but ultimately what we receive is ourselves.

This we must accept, not just without grumbling, without inward protest, but with a good will, because it is given to us by the God who asks: "Do you begrudge my generosity?" This, then, is our great life's work: to accept ourselves as the mysterious and gradually revealed gift of the eternal generosity of God. For everything that we are and have, even the painful and mysterious, is God's generous gift; we must not grumble at it but must accept it in the knowledge that when we do so God gives himself with his gift—here again the parable falls short of the reality—and so gives us everything that we could receive. To do this is the wisdom and the chief work of a Christian life. If we look into our own lives we will find that we have not always done it. All of us, young and old alike, are really latecomers. And yet God is willing to give us everything if we will only accept it—ourselves and himself and life without end.

(*Biblical Homilies,* 22-25)

Karl Rahner (1901-1984), a Swabian by birth, entered the Society of Jesus in 1922 and was ordained ten years later. After completing his studies at Freiburg and Innsbruck he was appointed to the theological faculty of Innsbruck in 1936. In 1949 he became a professor of dogmatic theology and in 1964 was appointed to a professorship in Munich. As a theological editor his name is associated with Denziger's *Enchiridion Symbolorum* and also with the *Lexikon für Theologie und Kirche* and *Sacramentum Mundi.* He was a peritus at Vatican II and the many volumes of *Theological Investigations* testify to his tireless labor as a theologian. Etienne Gilson drew attention to Rahner's "combination of intellectual modesty and audacity." A theologian of penetrating insight, he was also without doubt a man of God.

Twenty-Sixth Sunday in Ordinary Time

Gospel: Matthew 21:28-32   Jesus said to the chief priests and the elders of the people, "What is your opinion? A man had two sons. He went and said to the first, 'My boy, you go and work in the vineyard today.'"

Commentary: Y. de Montcheuil

*I*t is not those who say to me, "Lord, Lord," who will enter the kingdom of heaven, but the person who does the will of my Father in heaven. There is only one sign of belonging to the kingdom: faithfulness to the will of God. *A man had two sons. He went and said to the first, "My boy, you go and work in the vineyard today." He answered, "I will not go," but afterward thought better of it and went. The man then went and said the same thing to the second who answered, "Certainly sir," but did not go. Which of the two did the Father's will?* This parable alludes in the first place to the Jews and the Gentiles; but it also applies to each one of us. We said "yes" when we recognized the legitimacy of God's law and promised to submit to it; but very often we go on living as before without troubling ourselves about the will of God. We think we live in the kingdom because our "yes" was once sincere yet the force of daily habit eludes the will of God who is calling us to the kingdom. Often perhaps his will and our action coincide, but when a discrepancy arises between his will and ours, it is the latter which carries the day; we obey our own wishes and whims.

Now life in the kingdom does not merely consist in putting one's name down for it. Entry into the kingdom requires of us a continuing and living desire to accept God's will for us at each moment of our life. It is a "yes" said over and over again. In practice though, it is our unfaithfulness which is repeated. In particular there is a way of escaping from the will of God while believing that we are doing it; it consists in confusing the reality of a thing with the thought or idea of it. We can consider something very profoundly, relish it, esteem it in our hearts and yet live quite differently. Because our minds are warped we fail to notice the gap between idea and reality. We cannot, however, settle down once and for all in the kingdom of God; if we are not seeking to enter it at every moment, we can slip out of it without noticing.

The kingdom is for each one of us the response to a personal call; it means clinging to the personal will of God which varies for each one and likewise varies according to our circumstances. God's plan seen from the human angle is not a law established once and for all but a will revealed gradually according to the needs of the Church and our personal capabilities. Indeed the kingdom is not a place where we can sit back and relax. We have to be always following Jesus without knowing beforehand where we are going, ready to discern what God is expecting of us now. We must, then, keep careful watch, wakeful, attentive, and yet peaceful, to discern this living and evolving will of God. His demands on us can make us grow; he can ask of us tomorrow what he did not ask yesterday and so these demands engage us constantly in new ways. We need to examine our motives in all we do in order to hold ourselves always in readiness before God. This peaceful concern is neither agitation nor instability. It is true faithfulness and it issues from love, for the only means of knowing God's will for oneself is to love it and to prefer it to one's own. He who wishes to do the will of God must be on the alert to see it.

(Le Royaume et ses exigences, 94-96)

Yves de Montcheuil (1899-1944), professor at the Catholic Institute of Paris, was executed by the army of occupation at the age of forty-five, as the chaplain of the free French of Vercors. His thought profoundly influenced the theology of his time. Among those whose invisible presence inspired the Second Vatican Council—such as a Newman or a Teilhard de Chardin—he might be said to be the one who, after Karl Adam Moelher, most oriented the awareness of the Church as a mystery and as the sacrament of Christ in the Constitution on the Church.

Twenty-Seventh Sunday in Ordinary Time

Gospel: Matthew 21:33-43 — Jesus said to the chief priests and the elders of the people, "Listen to another parable. There was a man, a landowner, who planted a vineyard; he fenced it round, dug a winepress in it, and built a tower; then he leased it to tenants and went abroad."

Commentary: J. Daniélou

From the time of Moses to the time of Solomon, the vine of Israel grew until it spread from the Lebanon to Egypt, and from the Jordan to the sea.

That is how God honored his promises. His hopes were all set upon this vine, that it should bear his grapes. This is the key-signature of the Song of the Vine, for its theme turns wholly upon the hopes that God has of man, the mystery of the divine expectations. Primarily, it is the response of Israel that was expected, for Israel was the vine of the Lord's planting, from which he looked to have grapes. But apart from the Hebrews, all mankind is involved in these transactions. The vine of Israel is a type or figure of each one among us. The whole drama of sacred history is in this contrast of man's unbelief and God's fidelity.

Just how far the chosen people would go in their ingratitude is shown by Saint Matthew in the parable of the wicked husbandmen: After waiting patiently for two thousand years, God at length sent his Son in person, to save his vine at all hazards, thinking: *At least they will respect him.* But now, after all God's disappointments throughout the Old Testament, we see the crowning disappointment of all; for where the prophets had failed, Christ himself was to fail. God's patience has been strained to its farthest limit in this tragedy of Christ, the Lord of the vineyard's own son, rejected by the husbandmen, crucified, treated by his own people as a stranger and an outcast. But from these lowest depths arises a sudden hope: *He will let out the vineyard to other vinedressers, who will pay him his due when the season comes.*

The tragedy of Good Friday, when Israel rejected him that was sent, becomes in God's plan the means whereby the vine planted in Israel was to break out in a new and vigorous growth. In fact, it was to bring forth for the first time the fruit expected of it. Now through the passion and resurrection of Christ stems the true and faithful vine. *I am the vine, you are its branches; if a man lives on in me, and I in him, then he will yield abundant fruit; separated from me, you can have no power to do anything.*

The whole burden of the story of the chosen people was that man is powerless to achieve for himself the result that God expects of him; the purpose of the story was to deepen man's desire and longing for the true vine. Then the true vine appeared, in the person of Jesus Christ. The grace of God bears its plenitude of fruit in him; God can rest for ever from his labors, now that human nature brings forth this incomparable harvest of holiness. The response which the people of Israel had never been able to give is now given in perfection by God himself in the manhood of Jesus Christ, of the seed of Israel. All God's pleasure is in Jesus Christ, his everlasting vine, the eternal source of satisfaction without end: *This is my beloved Son, in whom I am well pleased.*

(*The Lord of History*, II, chapter 2, 170-171.177-180)

Jean Daniélou (1905-1974), born into a privileged family, his father being a politician and his mother an educationalist, did brilliantly at his studies, and in 1929 entered the Society of Jesus. He came under the influence of de Lubac and got to know Teilhard de Chardin. In 1940 he was chaplain to students in Paris and committed to the cause of resistance. Widely ecumenical in his views, he was a peritus at Vatican II under Pope John XXIII, and was made a cardinal by Pope Paul VI. As an author he was at home in many fields of erudition, including scripture, patristics, theology, and spirituality.

Twenty-Eighth Sunday in Ordinary Time

Gospel: Matthew 22:1-14

Jesus said to the chief priests and the elders of the people: "The kingdom of heaven may be compared to a king who gave a feast for his son's wedding. He sent his servants to call those who had been invited, but they would not come."

Commentary: R. Knox

*I*t is not difficult to see, it cannot, even when the parable was first uttered, have been difficult to see what our Lord was hinting at. The guests who first accept the invitation, and then disappoint their host at the last moment—who can they be but the Jews, the Pharisees in particular, to whom our Lord is speaking? God has planned a great banquet for them—all the spiritual riches of the Church, if they will have them. And that banquet is also a wedding feast; for its origin and its inspiration is that ineffable union between God's nature and man's which took place at the incarnation. That hope of redemption the Jewish people have made their own; they have looked forward to it through long centuries of unique and providential history. And now the moment of destiny has arrived; the preaching of our Lord and his apostles tells them that all things are now ready; the Church of the new covenant waits for them; they have only to come. And the invited guests revoke the acceptance they have given. Worldliness, in one form or another, has killed their appetite for the celestial delicacies so long promised to them, and with one consent they begin to make excuses. What remains to be done? What remains, but that almighty God should send out his neglected summons to the Gentile world instead, and recall the Gentiles, poor, blind, crippled after all those centuries of wandering away from him, to enter into the inheritance which his own chosen people has refused?

The highways and the hedges, the streets and the lanes of the city, the poor and the lame and the blind—that means you and me. Who were we, what were we, as God foresaw our lives in his inscrutable providence, that he should call us into the fellowship of his holy Catholic Church? There was nothing in ourselves that could attract him; there was no claim we could make upon his consideration; there was no added glory that our homage or our gratitude could bring to him, our Creator; we were creatures, and fallen. It was not simply that we were homeless, ever since we were banished from our appointed paradise; we were helpless too, groping in the dark with limbs that could scarcely carry us. His creatures, and his fallen creatures, God called us to himself; in utter condescension, in generosity for which we can never make return. He has made us children of his Church, and has set before us a banquet of spiritual delights, which is also a marriage feast.

(The Pastoral Sermons of Ronald Knox, 311-312)

Ronald Knox (1881-1951), son of E. A. Knox, one-time bishop of Manchester, England, was educated at Eton and Oxford. Already noted for the brilliance of his mind, he was appointed chaplain of Trinity College, Oxford, and became a leading figure among Anglo-Catholics. In 1917 he was received into the Roman Catholic Church and ordained two years later. He taught for a time at Saint Edmund's Ware and was chaplain to the Catholic undergraduates at Oxford from 1936 to 1939. At the request of the hierarchy he then devoted himself to making a new English translation of the entire bible. The New Testament was first published in 1945 and the Old in 1949. As a writer on a wide range of subjects, Knox's thought is often strikingly original and his style characterized by wit.

Twenty-Ninth Sunday in Ordinary Time

Gospel: Matthew 22:15-21   The Pharisees went away to work out between them how to trap Jesus in what he said. And they sent their disciples to him, together with the Herodians, to say, "Master, we know that you are an honest man and teach the way of God in an honest way."

Commentary: F. Sheen

A great hush must have come over the crowd at that moment as they saw the coin laying there in the hand of our Blessed Lord. Not many days hence, he who was the King of kings would have those very hands pierced by the nails under the orders of the representative of the man at whose portrait he looked. Our Lord asked them: *Whose is this likeness? Whose name is inscribed on it?* They answered: *Caesar's.* Then came his answer: *Why then, give back to Caesar what is Caesar's, and to God what is God's.* Our Lord took no sides, because the basic question was not God or Caesar, but God and Caesar. That coin used in their daily marketings showed they were no longer independent from a political point of view. In that lower sphere of life, the debt to the government should be discharged. He fostered no aspirations for independence; he promised no aid in liberation. It was even their duty to acknowledge the present dominion of Caesar, *imperante Tiberio.* The Greek word in the gospel for "give back" or "render" implied a moral duty such as Paul later on told the Romans, *imperante Nerone: Every soul must be submissive to its lawful authorities; authority comes from God only, and all authorities that hold sway are to his ordinance.* But in order to remove the objection that service to the government exempted from service to God, he added: *And to God what is God's.*

Once again he was saying that his kingdom was not of this world; that submission to him is not inconsistent with submission to secular powers; that political freedom is not the only freedom. To the Pharisees who hated Caesar came the command: *Give unto Caesar*; to the Herodians who had forgotten God in their love of Caesar came the basic principle: *Give unto God*. Had the people rendered to God his due, they would not now be in their present state of having to render too much to Caesar. He had come primarily to restore the rights of God. As he told them before, if they sought first the kingdom of God and his justice, all these things such as political freedom would be added unto them.

That coin bore the image of Caesar, but whose image did the questioners bear? Was it not the image of God himself? It was this image he was interested in restoring. The political could remain as it was for the time being, for he would not lift a finger to change their coinage. But he would give his life to have them render unto God the things that are God's.

(Life of Christ, 209-210)

_____

Fulton J. Sheen (1895-1979), born and educated in El Paso, Illinois, USA, was ordained in 1919 and continued his philosophical and theological studies in Washington, DC, Louvain, and Rome. Appointed professor of philosophy of religion at The Catholic University of America, Washington, DC, he did not lose touch with people of simpler minds, but retained his gift as a popular preacher. He was especially well known for his radio and television talks. His numerous books include: *God and Intelligence*, *The Philosophy of Science*, *The Eternal Galilean*, and *The Mystical Body of Christ*.

Thirtieth Sunday in Ordinary Time

Gospel: Matthew 22:34-40

When the Pharisees heard that Jesus had silenced the Sadducees they got together and, to disconcert him, one of them put forth a question, "Master, which is the greatest commandment of the law?"

Commentary: Teresa of Jesus

The Lord asks only two things of us: love for his Majesty and love for our neighbor. It is for these two virtues that we must strive, and if we attain them perfectly we are doing his will and so shall be united with him. But, as I have said, how far we are from doing these two things in the way we ought for a God who is so great! May his Majesty be pleased to give us grace so that we may deserve to reach this state, as it is in our power to do if we wish.

The surest sign that we are keeping these two commandments is, I think, that we should really be loving our neighbor; for we cannot be sure if we are loving God, although we may have good reasons for believing that we are, but we can know quite well if we are loving our neighbor. And be certain that, the farther advanced you find you are in this, the greater the love you will have for God; for so dearly does his Majesty love us that he will reward our love for our neighbor by increasing the love which we bear to himself, and that in a thousand ways, this I cannot doubt.

When I see people very diligently trying to discover what kind of prayer they are experiencing and so completely wrapped up in their prayers that they seem afraid to stir, or to indulge in a moment's thought, lest they should lose the slightest degree of the tenderness and devotion which they have been feeling, I realize how little they understand of the road to the attainment of union. They think that the whole thing consists in this. But no, sisters, no; what the Lord desires is works. If you see a sick woman to whom you can give some help, never be affected by the fear that your devotion will suffer, but take pity on her: if she is in pain, you should feel pain too; if necessary, fast so that she may have your food, not so much for her sake as because you know it to be your Lord's will. That is true union with his will.

Again, if you hear someone being highly praised, be much more pleased than if they were praising you; this is really easy if you have humility; for in that case you will be sorry to hear yourself praised. To be glad when your sisters' virtues are praised is a great thing, and, when we see a fault in someone, we should be as sorry about it as if it were our own and try to conceal it from others.

I have said a great deal about this elsewhere, sisters, because I know that, if we were to fail here, we should be lost. May the Lord grant us never to fail, and, if that is to be so, I tell you that you must not cease to beg his Majesty for the union which I have described. It may be that you have experienced devotion and consolations, so that you think you have reached this stage, and even enjoyed some brief period of suspension in the prayer of quiet, which some people always take to mean that everything is accomplished. But, believe me, if you find you are lacking in this virtue, you have not yet attained union. So ask our Lord to grant you this perfect love for your neighbor, and allow his Majesty to work, and, if you use your best endeavors and strive after this in every way that you can, he will give you more even than you can desire. If the opportunity presents itself, too, try to shoulder some trial in order to relieve your neighbor of it. Do not suppose that it will cost you nothing or that you will find it all done for you. Think what the love which our Spouse had for us cost him, when, in order to redeem us from death, he died such a grievous death as the death of the cross.

(*Interior Castle*, 261-263)

Teresa of Jesus (1515-1582) was born in Avila, Spain, and entered the Carmelites at eighteen years of age. She struggled with living the religious life, especially her prayer life, but grace finally won in 1555 when she resolved to give herself seriously to prayer and the life of perfection. She succeeded in inspiring the reform of the Carmelites with a vigorous apostolic spirit and in guiding her religious in the most lofty paths of prayer. Her writings were edited by her friend, Luis de León, O.S.A. In 1970 Pope Paul VI declared her a doctor of the Church.

Thirty-First Sunday in Ordinary Time

Gospel: Matthew 23:1-12

Addressing the people and his disciples Jesus said: "The scribes and the Pharisees occupy the chair of Moses. You must therefore do what they tell you and listen to what they say; but do not be guided by what they do: since they do not practice what they preach."

Commentary: J. Bossuet

Christ is our only real teacher. Unless we listen to his voice speaking within us, no teacher or preacher will be able to lead us to the truth.

To understand well what kind of attention you should give to the divine word, you need to be deeply impressed with the following Christian truth: besides the sound that strikes the ear, there is a secret voice speaking within, and this spiritual and interior teaching is the real instruction, without which all that human words can say is but a vain echo.

The Son of God does not allow us to assume the title of master. Let no one call himself master, he says, for there is only one master and one teacher. If we take this word to heart we realize that none but God can really teach us. Neither men nor angels have the power to do so; they can indeed tell us the truth, they can point it out, as it were, with their finger, but only God can teach it, only his light can enable us to distinguish one object from another.

If the sun were not shining, it would be useless for someone to show us the paintings inside a church and trace their contours with his finger; in vain would he expatiate upon the delicate line and rich coloring, as we should be unable to see anything. In the same way, among the many concepts claiming our attention, however much our instructor strove to distinguish between true and false, we should never be able to sift them aright, did not our intellect receive an invisible ray from him of whom it is written that he *enlightens every human being that comes into this world.*

Only in his light can we differentiate correctly; it is he who gives us a certain sense, called "the sense of Jesus Christ," enabling us to savor what is of God. It is he who opens the heart and says inwardly: You are listening to the truth. But the inner revelation is the real preaching. The ear receives the sound of the words, but the Teacher is within. Someone speaks from the pulpit, but the actual preaching is heard in the heart. For there is only one Master, Jesus Christ, and he alone teaches his people.

(*Oeuvres choisies*, 114-116)

Jacques Benigne Bossuet (1627-1704), outstanding Churchman and orator, was born at Dijon. As the fifth son of the family he was destined for the Church from an early age and was educated at Dijon, Metz, and at the Collège de Navarre in Paris. Saint Vincent de Paul prepared him for his ordination to the priesthood in 1652. Seven years later he took up residence in Paris where his fame as a preacher spread rapidly; his funeral orations evoked especial admiration. In 1669 he was appointed bishop of Condom, and in the following year was entrusted with the education of the Dauphin for whom, among other works, his *Discours sur l'histoire universelle* was written. In 1681 he was transferred to the see of Metz: it was for the religious in his charge that the *Méditations sur l'Evangile* and the *Elevations sur les mystères* were written. Among his voluminous writings 137 sermons have been preserved.

Thirty-Second Sunday in Ordinary Time

Gospel: Matthew 25:1-13   Jesus told this parable to his disciples: "The kingdom of heaven will be like this: Ten bridesmaids took their lamps and went to meet the bridegroom."

Commentary: R. Challoner

*T*he great lesson designed for us in this parable of the ten virgins is expressed in those words with which our Lord concludes: *Watch because you know not the day nor the hour.* The bridegroom in the parable came *in the middle of the night;* that is, at a time when he was least expected; according to what he has often signified, that he shall come *like a thief in the night,* and that we shall not know the hour of his coming. Not that he desires to surprise us; for if he did, he would not so often warn us; but that he desires we should *always watch,* and be always ready, that so we may never be surprised. *What I say to you,* he said to his disciples, *I say to all: watch.* And again: *Blessed are those servants whom the Lord, when he comes, shall find watching: Amen I say to you, that he will gird himself and make them sit down to eat, and passing he will minister unto them.*

O, who can express or conceive the greatness of these heavenly rewards, of these highest honors, of these never-ending joys, signified here by our Lord's ministering, in this manner, himself to the servants, whom he shall *find watching!* But O, the dismal case, on the other hand, of all them that, instead of watching, and being always ready, are *quite asleep* as to all that relates to God and their souls; and are not awakened, either with the love or fear of God, until death opens their eyes, when it is too late; and then, like the foolish virgins, they find the door shut against them, and are sent away, with *I know you not,* into the exterior darkness.

Conclude to bear always in mind this indispensable duty of watching, so frequently inculcated by the Son of God, that so you may never be surprised and *sleep in death*. Carry always with you the lamp of faith to enlighten yourself, but never forget that this light must be kept in with the oil of good works.

(*Meditations for Every Day in the Year*, 237)

Richard Challoner (1691-1781) was born at Lewes in Sussex, England. He studied at the English College of Douay and was ordained in 1716. After having received his doctorate in 1730 he was sent to the English missions. In the midst of his apostolic labors he found time to write and also to revise Gregory Martin's Douay Bible. At seventy years of age he was named titular bishop of Debre and served in the London district until his death.

Thirty-Third Sunday in Ordinary Time

Gospel: Matthew 24:14-30

Jesus spoke this parable to his disciples: "The kingdom of heaven is like a man on his way abroad who summoned his servants and entrusted his property to them. To one he gave five talents, to another two, to a third one; each in proportion to his ability."

Commentary: R. Challoner

Our Lord in the parable of the talents likens himself to a man going into a far country, who called his servants, and delivered to them his goods. To one he gave five talents, and to another two, and to another one; to everyone according to his proper ability; and immediately he took his journey. Our Lord by his ascension is gone into heaven, a far country indeed, from this wretched earth on which we dwell. But *ascending on high, he led captivity captive; he gave gifts to men.* He has plentifully distributed his goods and talents among his servants, to the end that they might trade with them and improve the stock during the time of his absence, till he shall come again and take an account of their good or evil management of their trust. He is the universal Lord of all; he distributes his talents amongst us all, according to his good pleasure. All whatsoever we have, as to soul or body, nature or grace, all belongs to him. We have nothing but what we have received from him, nor anything but what we are accountable for to him. And those that have received more than their neighbors have nothing to be proud of, for *what you have,* says the Apostle, *you have not received? And if you have received it, why do you glory?* On the contrary, those that have received more ought to be so much the more humble and to fear so much the more, because they are accountable for so much the more; for where more is given, more will be required.

Consider the different use that these servants made of their master's money. For *he that had received five talents went his way and traded* with the same, and gained another five. And in like manner, he that had received the two gained another two. But he that had received the one, going his way, digged in the earth and hid his lord's money. The two former are proposed for our imitation, that by the like industry in corresponding with divine grace and employing in a proper manner all the gifts of God, and laying hold on every opportunity of good, we may continually advance in virtue, and like these good and faithful servants, we may improve and double our stock. O how happy shall we be, if we shall trade in this manner with the talents committed to our charge! And though one of these servants gained five talents and the other but two, yet, as the latter who had received but two, was no less industrious than the former, gaining as much in proportion as he, so as to double his stock as well as he, we find him rewarded in like manner, and the same eulogium given to him by his master: *Well done, thou good and faithful servant; because thou hast been faithful over a few things, I will set thee over many things; enter thou into the joy of thy Lord.* O what encouragement is here for those who have received fewer talents, since we see, if they make proper use of what they have received, they shall be rewarded equally with them that have received more! But O the sublime reward that is here set before us in these words, *Enter thou into the joy of thy Lord.* For what is this joy of our Lord? Nothing less than the everlasting possession of himself—an universal, incomprehensible, eternal Good!

(*Meditations for Every Day in the Year,* 237-239)

Richard Challoner (1691-1781) was born at Lewes in Sussex, England. He studied at the English College of Douay and was ordained in 1716. After having received his doctorate in 1730 he was sent to the English missions. In the midst of his apostolic labors he found time to write and also to revise Gregory Martin's Douay Bible. At seventy years of age he was named titular bishop of Debre and served in the London district until his death.

Christ the King
Thirty-Fourth Sunday in Ordinary Time

Gospel: Matthew 25:31-46   Jesus said to his disciples: "When the Son of Man comes in his glory, escorted by all the angels, then he will take his seat on his throne of glory. All the nations will be assembled before him and he will separate men from one another as the shepherd separates sheep from goats."

Commentary: E.-J. de Smedt   *H*umanity seeks progress and happiness. It is a universal urge. The way to pursue this is clearly indicated by the law written in the natural tendencies of all creation. By calling it into existence, God has given to every being the law of balance and unity. Every individual creature seeks to preserve its unity. Every inferior being is oriented toward a high order, and is destined to the service of humanity. Men and women are called upon freely to achieve the balance and harmony of their natural tendencies, to subject them to reason, and to advance with all toward every great consciousness and unity. People cannot achieve real happiness unless they bring their actual conduct into line with the plan of the creator until, after their earthly probation, they will be finally united to their last end, God.

This equilibrium is endangered by sin, whose essence it is to destroy humanity's unity. Rebellion against God's plans brings about humanity's enslavement to matter and to its passions. This is soon enough followed by pangs of conscience, disruption of the family, insecurity, social conflicts, wars, and the break with God.

As you know, Jesus came to restore the unity that had been destroyed. His mission was the re-establishment of the created order's orientation toward its creator, the raising up of fallen humankind, and the restoration of union between humanity and God. But the work entrusted to Jesus by his Father does not stop there. The Son of God

142

was to open up new possibilities to humankind and to the world. Men and women were called to be sons and daughters of God, to live in Christ, to find a place in a mystical society of which Jesus would be the head, and which would be the family of God, the people of God. But it was not only to men and women that Christ would communicate his life: he was also, in a way, to confer it on all things. All creation was to be directed toward this divine end. Step by step it was to recover the order that was willed by the creator, until it would finally serve human beings as a springboard that would enable them to reach their ultimate destiny.

In this way was the new order to come about, *this his good pleasure God purposed in him, to be dispensed in the fullness of the times: to re-establish all things in Christ, both those in the heavens and those on earth.*

This is the kingship of Christ. The essence of royal power is not subject to others. Its prerogative is to orient persons and things toward the ends it proposes to attain. Jesus has merited this power as head and savior of humanity. He has the royal power of making laws destined to transform fallen creation; he exercises executive power and will pronounce final sentence at the end of time. After having merited this power by his life on earth, Jesus will effectively establish it by having all creation share, step by step, in his resurrection and in his glorification in heaven.

Christ appeals to the whole priestly community of his chosen people to spread his kingdom effectively throughout creation. He wishes to establish his kingship through you. By collaboration with Jesus in freeing yourselves from the chains of sin, you establish the rule of Christ.

(Priesthood of the Faithful, 41-44)

Emile-Joseph de Smedt was bishop of Bruges in Belgium. During the Second Vatican Council he was a member of the Secretariat for Christian Unity. At the Council he delivered some marvelous interventions on reform, unity, and doctrine.

Presentation of the Lord

Gospel: Luke 2:22-40
When the day came to purify them according to the law of Moses, the couple brought Jesus up to Jerusalem so that he could be presented to the Lord.

Commentary: John Paul II

Forty days after the nativity the Church celebrates an event full of spiritual significance. On that day the Son of God, as a tiny child of poor parents, born in a rough stable in Bethlehem, was carried to the temple in Jerusalem. This was his own temple, the temple of the living God, but he came to it not as the Lord but as one under the law. For the poor the law prescribed that forty days after the birth of the firstborn two turtle-doves or two young pigeons must be offered in sacrifice, as a sign that the child was consecrated to the Lord.

The message which the Spirit of God allowed the old man Simeon to sense and express so wonderfully was implicitly in the event itself, in this first encounter between the Messiah and his temple. On seeing the child, Simeon begins to utter words that are not of human provenance. He prophesies, prompted by the Holy Spirit; he speaks with the voice of God, the God for whom the temple was built and who is its rightful master.

Simeon's words begin, in what the liturgy calls the Song, by bearing witness to the light, and in so doing they ante-date by thirty years the witness borne by John the Baptist. They end, on the other hand, by bearing the first witness to the cross, in which contradiction of Jesus, the Christ, is to find tangible expression. The cost of the cross was shared by the mother, whose soul—according to Simeon's words—was to be pierced by a sword, *so that the thoughts of many hearts may be laid bare.*

Chronologically the presentation of Jesus in the temple is linked with the nativity, but in its significance it belongs with the mystery of the pasch. It is the first of the events which clearly reveal the messianic status of the newborn child. With him are linked the fall and the rising of many in the old Israel and also the new. On him the future of humankind depends. It is he who is the true Lord of the ages to come. His reign begins when the temple sacrifice is offered in accordance with the law, and it attains full realization through the sacrifice on the cross, offered in accordance with an eternal plan of love.

(Sign of Contradiction, 40-41)

John Paul II (1920-   ), born Karol Wojtyla, was ordained a priest in 1946, a bishop in 1958, made a cardinal in 1967, and elected pope in 1978. Hewn from the colossus of Polish Catholicism, formed by the discipline of study and manual labor, his physical, moral, and intellectual strength has been the rock on which the grace of God has built up the Church during a period of consolidation after Vatican II. His particular insights into the human condition, shaped by his interest in the theater, his gifts for poetry and play writing, and his study of personalist philosophy, have contributed much to the teaching of the Church.

Saints Peter and Paul

Gospel: Matthew 16:13-19   When Jesus had appeared to his disciples and had eaten with them, he said to Simon Peter, "Simon, son of John, do you love me more than these?" "Yes, Lord," Peter said, "you know that I love you." At which Jesus said, "Feed my lambs."

Commentary: J. Bonsirven   *I*n Palestine, the only solid foundation people knew was rock—*Kepha* in Aramaic. Simon, son of John, was to be this foundation. By this metaphor, an exalted rank in the Church, the primacy, was assigned to Peter, and its rights and prerogatives would become apparent as they were exercised. Paul, when he speaks of Christ as the chief cornerstone in the edifice of the Church, does not hesitate to call the apostles and the prophets the foundation on which the Church is built. There are some words of his which bear witness to the fact that the early Christians called Simon *Kepha* and acknowledged that his was a position of real primacy.

This was the first time Jesus mentioned his Church. Like Christ himself and all that he was doing, the Church was to be the target for the attacks of hostile powers represented here by "the gates of Hades," Hades being thought of then as the abode of the wicked, while in poetic style the gates designated a fortress. The satanic powers would not prevail against either the society or the rock which upheld it. The reign of God continued to triumph over the devil. In fact, the phrases which follow seem to identify the Church with the reign of God; Jesus has the power of a ruler in both of them. He appointed Peter Grand Vizier, the governor of the kingdom. His extensive power is symbolized by the keys, which the master of the house withdrew and handed over to his true servant. This authority is also indicated by the power to "bind and loose," words used in the rabbinical vocabulary to designate the power of the judiciary and the legislature.

The primacy of Peter is once again implied in the promise made to him on the eve of the passion. This event is compared with the act of sifting corn; only the good grain remains in the riddle: all the rest, straw, bad grain, soil, is thrown out. In the same way, the faith of the apostles was to be violently disturbed by the great ordeal. Their leader would not be overcome completely, and once he had returned to his original loyalty, would strengthen his brethren and direct them in their faith.

Peter was confirmed in his dignity later by our Lord after his resurrection—it was after his triumph that the Church was to show signs of autonomous life. We know the dialogue which was exchanged on the banks of the Sea of Tiberias amid the splendor of the rising sun. The Master wanted to make it clear to Simon by his thrice-repeated question that his office demanded a greater degree of love: the leader, more than anyone, must share the infinite charity of the supreme head. His official title was "shepherd." God called himself the shepherd of his people and gave the same title to the prophets, and especially to the Messiah. Jesus also described himself as the "good shepherd," proving his love for his flock by the sacrifice of his life. He made Peter his colleague and deputy in this pastoral ministry, which included the care and direction of the faithful.

(*The Theology of the New Testament*, 66-69)

Joseph Bonsirven (1880-1958), after his education and ordination at the Sulpician seminary in Paris, was assigned to teach scripture at the major seminary of Albi. In 1906 he studied at the École Biblique under Père Lagrange; in 1909 he received his licentiate in sacred scripture from the Pontifical Biblical Commission. The following year his doctoral thesis on rabbinic eschatology was not accepted, and he was forbidden to teach scripture. Bonsirven humbly accepted the decision and returned to his diocese for pastoral work, which was interrupted by service and subsequent imprisonment in World War I. While a prisoner of war, he was appointed by Benedict XV to teach dogmatic theology and scripture to imprisoned seminarians. After the war he joined the Society of Jesus and returned to teaching New Testament exegesis in France and then in Rome at the Biblical Institute.

Transfiguration of the Lord

Gospel: Matthew 17:1-9

Jesus took Peter, James, and his brother John and led them up a high mountain by themselves. He was transfigured before their eyes. His face became as dazzling as the sun, his clothes as radiant as light.

Commentary: J. Corbon

What took place in this unexpected event? Why did the Incomprehensible One allow his "elusive beauty" to be glimpsed for a moment in the body of the world? Two certainties can serve us as guides. First, the change, or, to transliterate the Greek word, the "metamorphosis," was not a change in Jesus. The gospel text and the unanimous interpretation of the Fathers are clear: Christ "was transfigured, not by acquiring what he was not but by manifesting to his disciples what he in fact was; he opened their eyes and gave these blind men sight." The change is on the side of the disciples. The second certainty confirms this point: the purpose of the transfiguration, like everything else in the economy that is revealed in the Bible, is the salvation of human beings. As in the burning bush, so here the Word "allows" the light of his divinity "to be seen" in his body, in order to communicate not knowledge but life and salvation; he reveals himself by giving himself and he gives himself in order to transform us into himself.

But if it be permissible to take off the sandals of curiosity and inquisitive gnosis and draw near to the mystery, we may ask: Why did Jesus choose this particular moment, these two witnesses and these three apostles? What was he, the Son—so passionately in love with the Father and so passionately concerned for us—experiencing in his heart? A few days before Peter had already been given an interior enlightenment and had acknowledged Jesus as the Christ of God. Jesus had then begun to lift the veil from the not far distant ending of his life: he had to suffer, be put to death, and be raised from the dead. It is between this first prediction and the second that he undertakes to ascend the mountain. The reason for the transfiguration can be glimpsed, therefore, in what the evangelists do not say: having finished the instruction preparatory to his own Pasch, Jesus is determined to advance to its accomplishment. With the whole of his being, the whole of his "body," he is committed to the loving will of the Father; he accepts that will without reservation. From now on, everything, up to and including the final struggle at which the same three disciples will be invited to be present, will be an expression of his unconditional "Yes" to the Father's love.

We must certainly enter into this mystery of committed love if we are to understand that the transfiguration is not an impossible unveiling of the light of the Word to the eyes of the apostles, but rather a moment of intensity in which the entire being of Jesus is utterly united with the compassion of the Father. During these decisive days of his life he becomes transparent to the light of the love of the One who gives himself to human beings for their salvation. The radiance of the light in the suffering body of Jesus is as it were the thrill experienced by the Father in response to the total self-giving of his only Son. This explains the voice that pierces through the cloud: "This is my Son, the Beloved; he enjoys my favor. Listen to him" (Mt 17:5).

(*The Wellspring of Worship*, 60-61)

Jean Corbon is a member of the Dominican community of Beirut and author of the book *L'Église des Arabes*. His whole thrust in writing on liturgy is to rediscover its meaning and to understand how the whole of life finds itself transformed.

Assumption of Mary

Gospel: Luke 9:39-56

Mary set out, proceeding in haste into the hill country to a town of Judah, where she entered Zechariah's house and greeted Elizabeth.

Commentary: L. Bouyer

Mary should be looked on as the living pledge of Christ's promises to the Church: that where he is, we also shall be; then the glory given him by the Father he will give to us, as he received it.

Consequently, it goes without saying that Mary's Assumption is, by no means, a kind of apotheosis dispensing her from the common human destiny, any more than the Immaculate Conception was an abnormal privilege designed to emancipate her from the conditions of human life. But, as Mary, by the grace of redemption brought by her Son, a grace to which, in opening herself, she opened the whole of humankind, was the first to be saved, and that more perfectly than any other person, as regards sin, so she is seen as saved the first and more perfectly than anyone else, as regards death, the result of sin. Her Immaculate Conception was the pledge of the perfect and wholly virginal purity to which, one day, the creature, sullied by sin, has to attain, in order to become the Spouse of Christ. Likewise, her Assumption is the pledge of the glory Christ will give to his spouse, as he has already given it to his mother. As John says: *It has not yet appeared what we shall be. We know that, when he shall appear, we shall be like to him, because we shall see him as he is.* For Mary, this condition is already realized. Her perfect faith passed, as it were, without any intermediate stage to sight. In the mother of Christ and our mother, we are given the pledge of his promise; seeing him as she sees him, we shall be like to her, who is already like to him. As Paul says: *We shall be taken up together to meet Christ, and so we shall always be with the Lord.*

How, then, are we to represent, as far as is possible, this state of glory, of eschatology already realized, to which Mary has entered in the train of her Son?

Christ's ascension does not mean that he has left us to our present condition, since he has gone only to prepare a place for us, that where he is we also may be; no more does Mary's assumption mean her separation from us. As her son is represented in the letter to the Hebrews as *always living to intercede for us,* so she remains, as the constant belief of the Church assures us, at his side, the interceder par excellence. Already her blessedness is perfect, present, as she is, with God who has placed in her his delight. But, more than ever, the contemplative prayer which raises her above the angels, in the bliss of an eternal eucharist, carries an irresistible intercession, on her part, that sinners, all of us countless children of hers, may come to be united to her in her Son.

(*The Seat of Wisdom,* 202-203)

Louis Bouyer (1913-), born in 1913 of Protestant parents, became a Lutheran minister until, as he says, "his profound studies into the nature of Protestantism as a genuinely spiritual movement led him gradually to the recognition that Catholicism was the only Church in which the positive elements of the Reformation could be exercised." He became a priest of the French Oratory and professor of spiritual theology at the *Institut Catholique* in Paris. He has written extensively on both ecumenism and liturgy.

Triumph of the Holy Cross

Gospel: John 3:13-17

No one has gone up to heaven except the one who came down from there—the Son of Man. Just as Moses lifted up the serpent in the desert, so must the Son of Man be lifted up, that all who believe may have eternal life in him.

Commentary: Anthony, Metropolitan of Sourozh

*T*he Lord himself has taken upon his shoulder the first cross, the heaviest, most appalling cross, but after him thousands and thousands of men, women, and children have taken upon themselves their own crosses, lesser crosses, but how often these crosses, which are lesser than Christ's, remain so frightening for us. Innumerable crowds of people have lovingly, obediently, walked in the footsteps of Christ, treading the long tragic way which is shown by our Lord, a way tragic but which leads from this earth to the very throne of God, into the kingdom of God. They walk, carrying their crosses, they walk now for two thousand years, those who believe in Christ. They walk on, following him, crowd after crowd, and on the way we see crosses, innumerable crosses, on which are crucified the disciples of Christ.

Crosses, one cross after the other, and however far we look, it is crosses and crosses again. We see the bodies of the martyrs, we see the heroes of the spirit, we see monks and nuns, we see priests and pastors, but many, many more people do we see, ordinary, simple, humble people of God who have willingly taken upon themselves the cross of Christ. There is no end to this procession. They walk throughout the centuries knowing that Christ has foretold us that they will have sorrow on this earth, but that the kingdom of God is theirs.

They walk with the heavy cross, rejected, hated, because of truth, because of the name of Christ. They walk, they walk, these pure victims of God, the old and young, children and grown-ups. But where are we? Are we going to stand and look; to see this long procession, this throng of people with shining eyes, with hope unquenched, with unfaltering love, with incredible joy in their hearts,

152

pass us by? Shall we not join them, this eternally moving crowd, that is marked as a crowd of victims, but also as little children of the kingdom? Are we not going to take up our cross and follow Christ? Christ has commanded us to follow him. He has invited us to the banquet of his kingdom, and he is at the head of the procession. Nay, he is together with each of those who walk. Is this a nightmare? How can blood and flesh endure this tragedy, the sight of all these martyrs, new and old? Because Christ is risen, because we do not see in the Lord who walks ahead of us the defeated prophet of Galilee as he was seen by his tormentors, his persecutors. We know him now in the glory of the resurrection. We know that every word of his is true. We know that the kingdom of God is ours if we simply follow him.

(*Meditations—A Spiritual Journey*, 123-125)

Anthony, Metropolitan of Sourozh (1914-), born Andre Borisovich Bloom in Lausanne, Switzerland, was educated at the Sorbonne, became a doctor of medicine before taking monastic vows in 1943 and became a priest of the Russian Orthodox Church in Paris in 1948. In 1960 he was ordained arch-bishop of Sourozh and then became in 1965 Metropolitan and Patriarch of Moscow and All Russia in Western Europe. He lectured in various parts of the world and authored many books on prayer and the spiritual life.

All Saints

Gospel: Matthew 5:1-12

When Jesus saw the crowds he went up on the mountainside. After he had sat down his disciples gathered around him, and he began to teach them: "Blessed are the poor in spirit; the reign of God is theirs."

Commentary: K. Adam

Hosts of the redeemed are continually passing into heaven, either directly or by the road of purification in the suffering Church. They pass into the presence of the Lamb and of him who sits upon the throne, in order face to face—and no longer in mere similitude and image—to contemplate the Trinity, in whose bosom are all possibilities and all realities, the unborn God from out of whose eternal well-spring of life all beings drink existence and strength, motion and beauty, truth and love. There is none there who has not been brought home by God's mercy alone. All are redeemed, from the highest seraph to the new-born child just sealed by the grace of baptism as it left the world. Delivered from all selfish limitations and raised above all earthly anxieties, they live, within that sphere of love which their life on earth has traced out for them, the great life of God. It is true life, no idle stagnation, but a continual activity of sense and mind and will. It is true that they can merit no longer, nor bear fruit now for the kingdom of heaven. For the kingdom of heaven is established and grace has finished its work. But the life of glory is far richer than the life of grace. The infinite spaces of the being of God, in all its width and depth, provide a source in which the soul seeks and finds the satisfaction of its most intimate yearnings. New possibilities continually reveal themselves, new vistas of truth, new springs of joy. Being incorporated in the most sacred humanity of Jesus, the soul is joined in most mysterious intimacy to the Godhead itself. It hears the heartbeats of God and feels the deep life that pulsates within the Divinity. The soul is set and lives at the center of all being, whence the sources of all life flow, where the meaning of all existence shines forth in the triune God, where all power and all beauty, all peace and all blessedness, are become pure actuality and purest present, are made an eternal now.

This life of the saints, in its superabundant and inexhaustible fruitfulness, is at the same time a life of the richest variety and fullness. The one Spirit of Jesus, their head and mediator, is manifested in his saints in all the rich variety of their individual lives, and according to the various measures in which every single soul, with its own special gifts and its own special call, has received and employed the grace of God. The one conception of the saint, of the servant of Christ, is embodied in an infinite variety of forms. The litany of the saints takes us rapidly through this "celestial hierarchy." And while every name denotes a special gift, a special character, a special life, yet all are united in one only love and in one gospel of joy and gladness.

(*The Spirit of Catholicism*, 120-122)

Karl Adam (1876-1966) was born in Bavaria, studied for the priesthood and was ordained in 1900. After some experience of pastoral work he taught first at the University of Munich and in 1918 became a professor at Strasbourg. A year later he was appointed to the chair of dogmatic theology at Tübingen, which he held until 1949. He was among the forerunners of ecumenism, liberal and up to date in thought, but always orthodox. His writings, which had great influence especially on the laity, include: *The Nature of Catholicism, Christ Our Brother,* and *The Son of God.*

All Souls

Gospel: Luke 7:11-17   Young man, I say to you, arise.

Commentary: Catherine of Genoa

There is no joy save that in paradise
to be compared with the joy of the souls in purgatory.
As the rust of sin is consumed
the soul is more and more open to God's love.
Just as a covered object left out in the sun
cannot be penetrated by the sun's rays,
in the same way,
once the covering of the soul is removed,
the soul opens itself fully to the rays of the sun.
Having become one with God's will,
these souls, to the extent that he grants it to them,
see into God.
Joy in God, oneness with him, is the end of these souls,
an instinct implanted in them at their creation.
All that I have said
is as nothing compared to what I feel within,
the witnessed correspondence of love
between God and the soul;
for when God sees the soul pure as it was in its origins,
he tugs at it with a glance,
draws it and binds it to himself with a fiery love.
God so transforms the soul in himself
that it knows nothing other than God.
He will not cease
until he has brought the soul to its perfection.
That is why the soul seeks to cast off
any and all impediments, so that it can be lifted up to God;
and such impediments

are the cause of the suffering of the souls in purgatory.
Not that the souls dwell on their suffering;
they dwell rather on the resistance they feel in themselves
against the will of God,
against his intense and pure love bent on nothing
but draw them up to him.
And I see rays of lightning
darting from that divine love to the creature,
so intense and fiery as to annihilate not the body alone
but, were it possible, the soul.
The soul becomes like gold
that becomes purer as it is fired,
all dross being cast out.
The last stage of love
is that which does its work without human doing.
If humans were to be aware
of the many hidden flaws in them
they would despair.
These flaws are burned away in the last stage of love.
God then shows the soul its weakness,
so that the soul may see the workings of God.
If we are to become perfect,
change must be brought about in us and without us;
that is, the change is to be the work not of human beings but of God.
This, the last stage of love,
is the pure and intense love of God alone.
The overwhelming love of God
gives the soul a joy beyond words.
In purgatory great joy and great suffering
do not exclude one another.

(*Purgation and Purgatory*, 71-82)

Catherine of Genoa (1447-1510) was married at the age of sixteen to Giuliano Adorno. After ten unhappy years she was suddenly converted to ardent love of God. Later her husband too was converted and helped her to care for the sick in a hospital at Genoa. Her teachings, compiled by others, are contained in *Purgation and Purgatory* and *The Spiritual Dialogue*.

Dedication of the Lateran Basilica

Gospel: Luke 19:1-10

Entering Jericho, Jesus passed through the city. There was a man there named Zacchaeus, the chief tax collector and a wealthy man. He was trying to see what Jesus was like, but being small of stature, was unable to do so because of the crowd.

Commentary: H. de Lubac

The mystery of the Church is our own mystery par excellence, for it is in his Church that God looks upon us and loves us, in her that he desires us and we encounter him, and in her that we cleave to him and are made blessed. She is the mountain visible from afar, the radiant city, the light set on a candlestick to illuminate the whole house. She is the "continual miracle" which is always announcing to people the coming of their Savior and manifesting his liberating power in examples without number; she is the magnificent vaulting under which the saints, like so many stars, sing together of the glory of the redeemer.

To a person who lives in her mystery she is always the city of precious stones, the heavenly Jerusalem, the bride of the Lamb, as she was to Saint John; and seeing her thus, he feels that very joy which bursts through the light-split skies of the Apocalypse and glows in its serene visions. One begins to understand what made Saint Augustine cry: "When I talk about her, I cannot stop."

Saint Clement of Alexandria said superbly, "Just as the will of God is an act, and is called the world, so also his intention is the salvation of all people, and is called the Church." So we should say of the Church, as of Christ, that her kingdom *shall be without end*, for the *nuptials of the Lamb* are eternal. For the elect salvation consists in being welcomed into the heart of the Church for which they were created, in which they have been predestined and are loved.

Holy Church has two lives, one in time and the other in eternity.

We must always keep a firm hold on the continuity of the one Church through the diversity of her successive states. Prior to the incarnation, before she had become the bride, she was the betrothed only; and that remains true to a certain extent until the end of time, in that the mystical marriage of Nazareth and Calvary needs the final parousia as its fulfillment. All the same, the Church has already received an incomparable betrothal gift, since her bridegroom has given her his very blood.

It is one and the same Church that is to see God face to face, bathed in his glory, and yet is our actual Church, progressing laboriously in our world, militant and on pilgrimage, humiliated daily in a hundred ways. In the depths of her being she is already the city of God; through the virtue of faith she has already been brought into the storerooms of the king. This holy Jerusalem is, mysteriously and in hope, the heavenly Jerusalem; our earthly mother is already our heavenly mother, and the doors which she opens to us are already the heavenly gates. There will be yet one more changing of brass into gold and iron into silver; but in and through this future transmutation she will always be "the same city of Yahweh, the Zion of holy Israel": "This is heavenly and that is heavenly; this is Jerusalem and that is Jerusalem." We ought, indeed, to love that very element in the Church which is transitory, but we ought to love it as the one and only means, the indispensable organ, the providential instrument; and at the same time as the pledge, the passing image, the promise of the communion to come.

(*The Splendor of the Church*, 25-54, passim)

Henri de Lubac (1886-1991), after the study of law, entered the Society of Jesus in 1913 at Saint Leonary in Great Britain and taught fundamental theology at the Catholic Faculty of Lyon. With Cardinal Daniélou he founded in 1940 the series *Sources Chrétiennes*. From 1960 onward he was a member of various Vatican commissions in preparation for the Council, and after the Council continued to work on various commissions. He was created a cardinal by Pope John Paul II in 1983. He authored numerous books and articles, his book *Catholicism* being his masterpiece. Cardinal de Lubac died in 1991.

Immaculate Conception

Gospel: Luke 1:26-38

The angel Gabriel was sent from God to a town of Galilee named Nazareth, to a virgin betrothed to a man named Joseph, of the house of David. The virgin's name was Mary. Upon arriving, the angel said to her: "Rejoice, O highly favored daughter, the Lord is with you. Blessed are you among women."

Commentary: R. Knox

The feast of our Lady's Immaculate Conception, which we celebrate today, is the promise and the earnest of Christmas; our salvation is already in the bud. As the first green shoot heralds the approach of spring, in a world that is frostbound and seems dead, so in a world of great sinfulness and of utter despair that spotless conception heralds the restoration of man's innocence. As the shoot gives unfailing promise of the flower which is to spring from it, this conception gives unfailing promise of the virgin birth. Life had come into the world again, supernatural life, not of man's choosing or of man's fashioning. And it grew there unmarked by human eyes; no angels sang over the hills to celebrate it, no shepherds left their flocks to come and see; no wise men were beckoned by the stars to witness that prodigy. And yet the first Advent had begun. Our Lady, you see, is the consummation of the Old Testament; with her, the cycle of history begins anew. When God created the first Adam, he made his preparations beforehand; he fashioned a paradise ready for him to dwell in. And when he restored our nature in the second Adam, once more there was a preparation to be made beforehand. He fashioned a paradise for the second Adam to dwell in, and that paradise was the body and soul of our blessed Lady, immune from the taint of sin, Adam's curse. It was winter still in all the world around; but in the quiet home where Saint Anne gave birth to her daughter, spring had begun.

Man's winter, God's spring; the living branch growing from the dead root; for that, year by year, we Christians give thanks to God when Advent comes round. It is something that has happened once for all; we look for no further redemption, no fresh revelation, however many centuries are to roll over this earth before the skies crack above us and our Lord comes in judgment. Yet there are times in history when the same mood comes upon us, even upon us Christians; the same mood of despair in which the world, Jewish and heathen, was sunk at the time when Jesus Christ was born. There are times when the old landmarks seem obliterated, and the old certainties by which we live have deserted us; the world seems to have exhausted itself, and has no vigor left to face its future; the only forces which seem to possess any energy are those which make for disruption and decay. The world's winter, and it is always followed by God's spring.

Behold, I make all things new, said our Lord to the saint of the Apocalypse; let us rejoice, on this feast of the Immaculate Conception, in the proof and pledge he has given us of that inexhaustible fecundity which belongs only to his grace. And let us ask our blessed Lady to win for us, in our own lives, that continual renewal of strength and holiness which befits our supernatural destiny. Fresh graces, not soiled by the memory of past failure; fresh enterprise, to meet the conditions of a changing world; fresh hope, to carry our burdens beyond the shifting scene of this present world into the changeless repose of eternity.

(*University and Plain Sermons*, 402-405)

Ronald Knox (1881-1951), son of E. A. Knox, one-time bishop of Manchester, England, was educated at Eton and Oxford. Already noted for the brilliance of his mind, he was appointed chaplain of Trinity College, Oxford, and became a leading figure among Anglo-Catholics. In 1917 he was received into the Roman Catholic Church and ordained two years later. He taught for a time at Saint Edmund's Ware and was chaplain to the Catholic undergraduates at Oxford from 1936 to 1939. At the request of the hierarchy he then devoted himself to making a new English translation of the entire bible. The New Testament was first published in 1945 and the Old in 1949. As a writer on a wide range of subjects, Knox's thought is often strikingly original and his style characterized by wit.

Acknowledgements

In an anthology of readings it is sometimes difficult to locate all the copyright holders of the individual readings selected. Over the years the copyright holder may have transferred the rights to another company, or the copyright has reverted to another entity. Also there are changes of address, for several requests have been returned.

If I have failed to acknowledge a copyright, please bring it to my attention, and a correction will take place. Thank you.

Abhishiktanada or Henri Le Saux, *Prayer*, 2d ed. (SPCK, 1973). Used by permission of the publishers.

Karl Adam, *The Spirit of Catholicism* (Düsseldorf: Patmos Verlag, GmbH).

Edward A. Armstrong, *The Gospel Parables* (Kansas City: Sheed and Ward).

Pedro Arrupe, S.J., *Justice with Faith Today* (reprinted by permission of the Institute of Jesuit Resources, St. Louis).

Anthony Bloom, *Meditations—A Spiritual Journey* (Denville: Dimension Books, 1971).

Dietrich Bonhoeffer, *The Cost of Discipleship*, translated from the German by R.H. Fuller, with some revisions by Irmgard Booth (SLM Press, Ltd., 1959). Reprinted by permission of Simon and Schuster.

Joseph Bonsirven, S.J., *The Theology of the New Testament* (Wellwood, England: Search Press Ltd–Burns and Oates, Ltd.).

Walter J. Burghardt, S.J., *Grace on Crutches: Homilies for Fellow Travelers*, ©1986 by Walter J. Burghardt, S.J. Used by permission of Paulist Press.

Odo Casel, O.S.B., *Gegenwart des Christus-Mysteriums* (Mainz: Matthias-Grünewald-Verlag, 1986).

Catherine of Genoa, *Purgation and Purgatory, The Spiritual Dialogue*, translated by Serge Hughes, ©1979 by the Missionary Society of Saint Paul the Apostle in the State of New York. Used by permission of Paulist Press.

Jean Corbon, *The Wellspring of Worship*, translated by Matthew O'Connell. English translation ©1988 by The Missionary Society of Saint Paul the Apostle in the State of New York. Used by permission of Paulist Press.

Jean Daniélou, S.J., *Jean-Baptiste, temoin de l'Agneau*, © Editions du Seuil (reprinted by permission of Georges Borchardt, Inc).

Francis X. Durwell, C.SS.R., *The Resurrection* (Kansas City: Sheed and Ward).

David E. Garland, *Reading Matthew: A Literary and Theological Commentary on the First Gospel*, ©1993 David E. Garland (reprinted by permission of The Crossroad Publishing Company, New York).

Romano Guardini, *The Lord* (South Bend: Regency Gateway).

Bernard Häring, C.SS.R., *The Beatitudes* (reprinted by permission of the author).

Monika Hellwig, *Jesus, the Compassion of God* (Collegeville: Michael Glazier–Liturgical Press).

Julian of Norwich, *Showings*, translated by Edmund College, O.S.A., and James Walsh, S.J., ©1975 by The Missionary Society of Saint Paul the Apostle in the State of New York. Used by permission of Paulist Press.

Martin Luther King, *Strength to Live*. Reprinted by arrangement with the Heirs to the Estate of Martin Luther King, Jr., c/o Joan Daves Agency as agent for the proprietor, ©1963 Martin Luther King, Jr., renewed ©1991 Coretta Scott King.

Henri de Lubac, S.J., *The Splendor of the Church* (Kansas City: Sheed and Ward).

Thomas Merton, *Meditations on the Liturgy* (Oxford: Mowbray).

Jean Mouroux, *The Christian Experience* (Kansas City: Sheed and Ward).

Johannes Pinsk, *Gedanken zum Herrenjahr* (Mainz: Matthias-Grünewald-Verlag, 1963).

Karl Rahner, S.J., *Biblical Homilies* (New York: Crossroad).

Béda Rigaux, O.F.M., *The Testimony of St. Matthew* (Chicago: Franciscan Herald Press).

Thérèse of Lisieux, *Story of a Soul*, translated by John Clarke, O.C.D., ©1975, 1976 Washington Province of Discalced Carmelite Friars, Inc. (Washington, D.C.: ICS Publications).

Gerald Vann, O.P., *The Eagle's Word*, ©1961 and renewed 1989 by Gerald Vann (reprinted by permission of Harcourt, Brace and Company).

Index of Scripture

Index of Authors

Also available from New City Press in the same series:

Journey with the Fathers
Commentaries on the Sunday Gospels

EDITH BARNECUT, O.S.B. (ed.)
Foreword by JOHN E. ROTELLE, O.S.A.

"Each Sunday Gospel is adorned with a reading from one of the early classic writers. The selection is appropriate not only for preparing homilies but also for prayerful meditation."
The Bible Today

"Special care has been taken in making the translations so they may be proclaimed effectively. There is a brief introduction to the life and ministry of each author included in the collection."
Worship

Year A
ISBN 1-56548-013-9, **2d printing**
paper, 5 3/8 x 8 1/2, 168 pp., $9.95

Year B
ISBN 1-56548-056-2, **2d printing**
paper, 5 3/8 x 8 1/2, 160 pp., $9.95

Year C
ISBN 1-56548-064-3, **2d printing**
paper, 5 3/8 x 8 1/2, 160 pp., $9.95